A JUNGIAN LEGACY
TOM KIRSCH

Edited by
LUIS MORIS

Foreword by
JEAN KIRSCH

CHIRON PUBLICATIONS • ASHEVILLE, NORTH CAROLINA

© 2019 by Chiron Publications. All rights reserved. No part of this publication may be reproduced, stored in a retrieval system, or transmitted, in any form by any means, electronic, mechanical, photocopying, recording, or otherwise, without the prior written permission of the publisher, Chiron Publications, P.O. Box 19690, Asheville, N.C. 28815-1690.

www.ChironPublications.com

Interior and cover design by Danijela Mijailovic
Printed primarily in the United States of America.

Cover image © Luis Moris

ISBN 978-1-63051-728-1 paperback
ISBN 978-1-63051-729-8 hardcover
ISBN 978-1-63051-730-4 electronic
ISBN 978-1-63051-731-1 limited edition paperback

Library of Congress Cataloging-in-Publication Data

Names: Moris, Luis, editor.
Title: A Jungian legacy : Thomas Kirsch / edited by Luis Moris.
Description: Asheville, N.C. : Chiron Publications, [2019] | Includes bibliographical references and index. | Summary: "From the moment of his conception in his mother womb, Tom Kirsch was surrounded by Jungians. Jungian psychology was, as it were, written into his DNA. His contributions to the field are immeasurable and his legacy will continue to impact future generations. In A Jungian Legacy: Tom Kirsch, Luis Moris has edited and published the complete text of a filmed interview with Tom and enlarged this manuscript with chapters by some of Tom's closest friends and colleagues"-- Provided by publisher.
Identifiers: LCCN 2019020256 | ISBN 9781630517281 (paperback) | ISBN 9781630517298 (hardcover)
Subjects: LCSH: Jungian psychology. | Jung, C. G. (Carl Gustav), 1875-1961. | Kirsch, Thomas, 1936-
Classification: LCC BF173 .J85 2019 | DDC 150.19/54--dc23
LC record available at https://lccn.loc.gov/2019020256

Table of Contents

Foreword — 5
by Jean Kirsch

Preface — 9
by Luis Moris

Introduction — 17
by Murray Stein

The Arch of My Life — 37
by Thomas B. Kirsch

Thomas B. Kirsch in Conversation with Murray Stein in the Home of C.G. Jung — 57
by Thomas B. Kirsch and Murray Stein

Thomas Kirsch: A Man for All Seasons — 97
by Thomas Singer

Tom as a Feeling Mentor and Monitor — 113
by John Beebe

Tom Kirsch in China — 131
by Gao Lan, Heyong Shen

Tribute to Tom Kirsch — 147
by Andreas Jung

Loving Tom, Living Tom, Losing Tom—a *Bricolage* — 153
by Andrew Samuels

About the Author — 165

Foreword
by Jean Kirsch

A cascade of synchronistic events brought this book to life. It all began in 2015, when Tom and I were trying to plan a celebration of his 80th birthday, which was to fall on June 14 of the following year. His great desire was to bring our family together in his beloved Switzerland, to share with them a bit of the country that had become the home of his heart and soul. For many reasons, it was not coming together as he wished, and we had resigned ourselves to the prospect of a small celebration among friends in San Francisco. That was our plan, until October 2015, when, at the 7th International China Conference in Macao, Ruth Ammann invited me to speak to the candidate group at the C.G. Jung Institute, Zurich, in June 2016. Her invitation was followed shortly after by an invitation to Tom to address the analysts and candidates of both the C.G. Jung Institute and the International School of Analytical Psychology, on June 6, 2016, at the annual Jung's Memorial Day.

Luis Moris, a young analytic candidate with experience directing and producing filmed interviews of professional quality, upon hearing this news, began to dream of a filmed interview of Tom. He approached Murray Stein with his idea for the project. Murray agreed enthusiastically and then approached our good friends, Andreas and Vreni Jung, about the possibility of doing the interview in their home at 228 Seestrasse in Küsnacht, the home that Andreas's grandfather C.G. Jung had built in 1907. They readily assented and a date was set. On June 7, 2016, one week before Tom's 80th birthday, he would be interviewed by Murray Stein in Jung's consulting room and the interview would be filmed by Luis Moris and his French colleague and cameraman, Franck Guillemain. Our children, David and Susannah, hearing this news said, "That sounds like fun! Can we crash the party?" Thus, Tom was to have his heart's desire fulfilled. We would celebrate his 80th birthday in Zurich and the Upper Engadin with all members of our immediate family!

On the day of June 7, the weather was perfect, the sun shining warmly on the lake of Zurich. Murray and his wife, Jan, Tom, and I arrived in the early morning. As we strolled up the pathway of 228 Seestrasse, the front door was flung open by Andreas, who waved and called a cheery greeting. Luis and Franck were already there. They had been filming around the perimeter of the house, and had chosen the best angles for the lighting in Jung's consulting room. After a round of greetings and brief preliminaries, the four principles climbed the stairs to closet themselves above. Jan, Vreni, Andreas, and I chatted on the veranda while the interview took place. At its conclusion, the six of us gathered for lunch at the nearby Hotel Sonne in Kusnacht, while Luis and Franck sped off with their film. Everyone was in an especially good mood that day. None of us knew what magic had occurred in Jung's inner sanctum.

FOREWORD

Something numinous and profound had to have taken place there, that day, among the four men cloistered in Jung's space. The evidence is in the film itself. Never, in all the years that I have known him, has Tom ever spoken with greater ease and honesty, or from a greater depth of his being, about what has had the greatest meaning for him. I can testify that it was a transformative moment for Tom and I believe that it might have been so for Luis Moris, too.

Luis has been motivated to edit and publish the complete text of the filmed interview herein and to enlarge this manuscript with chapters by some of Tom's closest friends and colleagues. Tears filled my eyes, as I read the table of contents. It is as if Tom's individuation process, which had seemed to unfold by a larger plan in the final 18 months of his life, has continued beyond death.

Our lives do live on in the minds and hearts of those who remember us. This book is a work of love, a kind of Kaddish, for which Tom may be deeply grateful.

Luis, thank you.

Jean Kirsch, October 22, 2018

Preface

by Luis Moris

The first time I saw Dr. Thomas Kirsch was at a book launch at the 2013 IAAP Congress in Copenhagen. One afternoon in a main hall, a rather large group of people formed a half circle around several speakers who were going to present their forthcoming books. Among the five or six speakers was Dr. Kirsch. As he started speaking, somehow, in a very strange and slow way, I felt myself becoming deeply moved by his presence. This was my introduction to Dr. Kirsch, but I did not really know who he was. I was in my second year of training to become an analyst at International School of Analytical Psychology (ISAP-Zurich) and did not know many analysts outside Switzerland and France. So, I was in front of a stranger, really, but something within me was deeply touched by this unknown man. His body movements surprised me: they were free and open, relaxed, undefended. His face looked tender, at times like a young boy, I felt, and his soft smile was constantly radiating warmth. I was also surprised by the way he was dressed, very casually, I remember thinking. I do not remember everything he said during his short talk, but I do remember that he made us all laugh with a steady stream of jokes. He looked like he was really enjoying being at the center of this circle, and at the same time he seemed humble and genuine to me. He looked as though he'd been around for a while, I thought.

Three years later, when I found out he was coming to Zurich on June 6th to give a talk for Jung's Memorial Day, an event organized each year by ISAP-Zurich and the C.G. Jung Institute from Zurich, I could hardly contain my excitement. During the three years that had passed, I had read some articles by Dr. Kirsch, and I had formed a better idea about the person I had listened to in Copenhagen. I thought: A film must be made of this man! But even though at the time I had already made many films of interviews with Jungian analysts from Zurich, I did not feel that I was the right person for the interview with Dr. Kirsch. I did not know him personally and had only had read about some of his significant life experiences in the Jungian world, while he had no idea who I was. So, I immediately thought of Murray Stein. I knew that Murray and Dr. Kirsch had enjoyed a long friendship, dating back to the years when they worked together at the IAAP.

I presented the idea to Murray in his office in Zurich and he liked the project right away. He suggested a location I would have never imagined asking for: the home of C.G. Jung! Not only was I surprised when later Murray told me that Andreas Jung, the grandson of C.G. Jung, had accepted the idea of making a film of Dr. Kirsch in his home, but I was even more astonished when I was invited by Andreas to come to his home to inspect the place of the interview.

Andreas received me with surprising warmth and openness. I was deeply touched and grateful for his trust. He suggested different places in his beautiful

PREFACE

home to stage the interview, but it was when we entered Jung's library that my whole body and soul decided with certainty that this was the place, Jung's library, where one hundred years earlier he had worked on *The Red Book*. Without a doubt, this was the place to have these two senior Jungian analysts speak with one another. In this place, I felt, the spirits still dwell.

Through emails, Dr. Kirsch and Murray started discussing the points they were going to talk about during the interview, and later Murray carefully informed me about these. I thought they were all very important subjects, and I made a couple of suggestions for other important topics that I as a young Jungian student from a different generation would like to hear him address.

The whole process of preparation for the interview was somehow very organic and very smooth. My first impressions of Tom's deep and special presence from three years earlier were confirmed, yet I was still astonished by his openness and warmth toward me and toward the project.

Franck Guillemain, a close friend and partner in filmmaking, and I recorded Tom's entire talk at ISAP-Zurich on June 6, 2016, and later made a film of his talk. The next day, June 7, exactly one week before Tom turned 80, we all met in the home of C.G. Jung in order to record the interview. I was quite anxious about the shooting; I had ideas for the introductory scene of the film, but I had to tell Murray and Tom, whose health was delicate at the time, to repeat certain scenes such as the one going upstairs several times. It all worked out well, with both Tom and Murray being very cooperative, and once again things simply ran smoothly.

As is clear in the film and also in the written transcript found in this book, the conversation of these two old friends became precisely that, a conversation between two old friends. They had both agreed on talking about certain themes from Tom's life, but the conversation was not restricted to these topics, and it took on a life of its own. Murray did a great job in structuring the conversation with his questions, and Tom did a great job in openly receiving them and responding in a spontaneous and genuine way. They spoke for about two and a half hours, with only one short pause that I suggested toward the end to make sure that no topic of importance had been forgotten or neglected. Tom told me later that at the end of the interview he was not feeling tired at all and that he could have kept on talking for a couple of hours more! He also told me that he so got engrossed in Murray's questions that he not only forgot about the cameras but also forgot he was in Jung's library!

Franck and I edited the interview, and a good friend and colleague from ISAP-Zurich, Rodney Waters, performed the music for the film. Even though I believe I kept the most important parts of the interview in the film, I thought that it would be a valuable contribution to the history of analytical psychology to have both Tom's lecture at ISAP-Zurich and his entire interview with Murray Stein in one book. That is how this book first began.

Soon after we released it, the film was viewed by different people around the world and I received emails from people unknown to me, friends of Tom, thanking me for having created it. Tom was very happy about

PREFACE

how the film had turned out, and together we started to organize a viewing of the film for the summer of 2017 at the San Francisco Jung Institute. My wife, Anina, and I arrived in San Francisco on August 9, 2017, for the viewing that was going to take place the day after. Unfortunately, the day before the screening of his film, Tom suffered from a sudden and strong breakdown that forced him to stay in bed. He could not attend to the viewing of the film, but Dr. Thomas Singer took his place and directed the conversation we had at the institute after the viewing. The room was full, and I was so touched by people's comments about the film and about Tom. It was clear to me that Tom had deeply touched the lives of a lot of people in that room. He is loved by many in San Francisco.

We visited Tom the day after the viewing in his home in Palo Alto. He had a bed placed in the living room, and he received me with a delicate yet warm and wide smile. We spoke for some time and I was surprised to realize that his mind and memory were as sharp as the year before when we first met for the interview. In that conversation he told me how sorry he was for not having been able to attend the viewing, and he asked me whether people had liked the film. He also told me how much he loved Zurich and spoke to me about his friendship with Robert Hinshaw and how important Christa Robinson had been for him in the last few years. I promised him, in the living room of his home, that I would finish and publish the book with his talk and interview from Zurich. He shook my hand, said goodbye and again warmly smiled. I came back to Zurich with the mission of publishing the book. Tom died two months after that, peacefully in his home.

    I soon realized, as I started to work on the book, that adding essays from close friends of Tom who would share how he touched their lives would enrich the book. He has left a legacy not only through his books and vast firsthand knowledge of analytical psychology, but also through these people. I first asked Murray to write an introduction, and his essay describes not only Tom's Jungian life, but also how the interview and preparation with Tom took place. After asking Murray, I also asked Andreas Jung for a contribution. His essay shows how Tom touched his life and the one of his wife, Vreni, by opening "The Gates to the World" to them. The essay of Tom Singer, who, like every single person I approached for this book project, immediately accepted the task, writes intimately about his friendship with and love for Tom and how he sees Tom's local and international contribution to analytical psychology. John Beebe's essay shows how Tom acted as a mentor to him when experiencing his feeling function and how gifted Tom was in dealing with conflicts in the international scene. Andrew Samuels' *Bricolage* shares three separate essays Andrew wrote for Tom during the period of his illness and after his death. His three pieces present a very unique way of having experienced Tom. Heyong Shen's contribution is a beautiful piece that demonstrates the long exchange there was between Tom and China, thanks to his "Chinese heart." The interview between Tom and Murray has been edited for this book just to make the reading smoother but none of its content has been altered. Nothing has been cut out, either. Tom's

PREFACE

lecture is exactly as he gave for Jung's Memorial Day at ISAP-Zurich on June 6, 2016.

By asking these people to contribute to this book, my aim was to show the diversity of perspectives there are about a man who was destined to become a Jungian analyst and great contributor to our field. Throughout the entire process of creating this book I was amazed by the love these analysts showed for Tom.

I would like to thank several people who have made both the film and this book possible. First, I would like to thank Jean Kirsch, who from the beginning has been a true supporter of this project. When I wondered why I, a young analyst who knew Tom for such a short time, was putting together such a book, she was the one who gave me the support I needed to continue with it. Without her, this book would have not seen light. Also, without the support of Tom Singer, Andrew Samuels, John Beebe, and Murray Stein, this book would have not existed. I would like to thank Wendy Willmot and Dr. Hao-Wei Wang for believing in the film project and contributing to its making. I would also like to once again thank Vreni and Andreas Jung for their trust and for allowing me to use images of their home in both the film and in this book. As mentioned earlier, a big thank you goes to Rodney Waters, who added depth to the images with his music for the film. I would also like to thank Steve Buser and Leonard Cruz from Chiron Publications for believing in these projects dedicated to Tom, and for supporting them from their inception. A big thank you, again, to Murray Stein, for his solid, warm, and enthusiastic support, for sharing his creativity with me, and for helping me so much with the technical details of how to put together a book. And last but certainly not least, I would like to thank my wife Anina- I could have literally not done these projects without her constant and loving support.

Luis Moris

Zurich, November 7, 2018

Introduction

by Murray Stein

A Biographical Sketch

From the moment of his conception in his mother womb, Tom Kirsch was surrounded by Jungians. Jungian psychology was, as it were, written into his DNA. The title of his autobiographical memoir, *A Jungian Life*,[1] says it well.

Thomas Basil Mordechai Kirsch[2] was born on June 14, 1936, in London, where his father, James Kirsch, had recently set up a Jungian analytical practice. James and Hilde Kirsch had migrated there from Tel Aviv where they had lived for three years after leaving Berlin following Hitler's rise to power. Jewishness would define their lives to a great extent, although they were not religious in a traditional sense. Tom's sense of identity was deeply rooted in this feeling of belonging to the Jewish people, its history and its present reality in the contemporary world. His first years were shadowed by the threat of annihilation, and much later in life he would speak of his recurrent memories of the bombing of London by Nazi aircraft. In 1940, the Kirsch family,

---

[1] Kirsch, Thomas B. (2014). *A Jungian Life*. Carmel, CA: Fisher King Press.
[2] For the meaning of these names, see Thomas Kirsch, *A Jungian Life*, 5. It's an interesting story and has significant meaning for Tom's identity.

fearing a Nazi takeover of England, fled to the United States, where they eventually settled in Los Angeles. (In London, incidentally, Michael Fordham, wishing to receive Jungian analysis and training, entered into analysis with Tom's mother at Jung's recommendation. He was her first analytical case!)

Once settled on the West Coast of America and out of reach of the threat of Germany, both parents set up analytic practices and began working with patients in the New World. (Hilde was by now becoming an accomplished Jungian analyst.) As Jungian pioneers in California, both parents became well known for their teaching and hospitality to visiting Jungians and other immigrants, and eventually they formed a group of followers that would become the C.G. Jung Institute of Los Angeles. Both parents were significant figures in the growing presence of Jungians on the West Coast in the 1940s and '50s. Growing up in this home of dedicated Jungians, Tom was more or less destined to become one, too. He would sometimes humorously remark that in becoming a Jungian analyst he was "joining the family business."[3] His half brother, James Silber, also became a Jungian analyst.

Tom's academic preparation for his long career in analytical psychology began rather tangentially with a bachelor's degree in French literature from Reed College (thesis topic: a study of *À la recherche du temps perdu* by Marcel Proust). This was followed by a more direct

---

[3] I once asked Tom what career he would have chosen had he not become a Jungian analyst, and he said he would go into research in endocrinology. He found the subject fascinating in medical school.

INTRODUCTION

route with a medical degree from Yale Medical School, psychiatric residency at Stanford University, and finally analytical training at the C.G. Jung Institute of San Francisco. His first analysis, begun when he a teenager, was with Jung's designated heir, C.A. Meier. During his analytic training in San Francisco he entered into a longstanding and profoundly transformative analysis with Joseph Henderson, with whom he maintained a close relationship until Henderson's death at the age of 104 in 2007. Henderson would become Tom's Jungian "godfather" and mentor. Rising quickly into positions of responsibility in his home institute, Tom was elected president of the Jung Institute in San Francisco in 1976 and served until 1980. In 1977, at the Congress in Rome, he was elected vice president of the IAAP. He would occupy a position on the IAAP Executive Committee for the next 18 years, the last six years as president.

Tom represented a pivotal generation in the field of analytical psychology as it evolved from a tightly knit circle of students trained directly by Jung and his immediate assistants in Zurich (primarily Emma Jung and Toni Wolff) to a far-flung international association (the IAAP) made up of analysts trained by Jung's students such as Joseph Henderson, C.A. Meier, M.-L. von Franz, Jolande Jacobi, Erich Neumann, Gerhard Adler, Michael Fordham, James Kirsch, Esther Harding, and a host of others. This first group of Jungian analysts was an outstanding generation made up of men and women with brilliant minds and a passion for teaching the practical applications of analytical psychology. They were the founders of the important training institutes in Europe, Israel, and the United States (Zurich, London,

New York, San Francisco, Los Angeles, Italy, France, Germany, and Israel). Following that group came Tom's generation, also outstanding in many respects and including such well known figures as Adolf Gugenbühl-Craig (a close personal friend of Tom's), James Hillman, Hayao Kawai, June Singer, Carlos Byington, Hans Dieckmann, Ellie Humbert and many others. This group carried on the work begun by their teachers and consolidated the training programs started earlier, adding features and practices that met the needs of the changing times and the various cultures in which they lived.

Tom's presidency of the IAAP (1989-1995) straddled the end of the Cold War and the opening of new parts of the world to Jungian thought, most notably in Russia and China. Tom became deeply involved in introducing the IAAP in these areas as people there began showing a strong interest in Jungian psychology and asking about ways to train as Jungian analysts. Among his initial efforts in this direction was a trip to what was, at the time, still the Soviet Union. In 1991, he traveled to Moscow to look into the possibility of having Jung's *Collected Works* translated into Russian. As it turned out, Tom arrived in Moscow during the episode that changed the course of history in that part of the world, the weekend that Boris Yeltsin faced down the coup against Gorbachev, which led to the resignation of the Communist politburo and the dissolution of the Soviet system. The project to translate Jung into Russian did begin as a result of his efforts, but it later collapsed in the financial chaos that erupted in Russia of the 1990s. Later, it was again taken up under more favorable circumstances.

INTRODUCTION

Following his presidency, Tom set out to write what would become his most important published work, *The Jungians*.[4] This carefully researched study describes the growth of Jungian groups throughout the world and demonstrates Tom's extensive knowledge of the history of the development of Jungian organizations in many lands. He visited most of the places he writes about in this book and knew the founding members and many of the analysts in these groups personally. The book, published in 2000, is exhaustive and has become a standard reference work in the field.

The next major project that occupied Tom was overseeing the publication of his father's extensive correspondence with Jung. James Kirsch had made contact with Jung by letter in 1928, and for the remainder of Jung's life they stayed in regular contact by post. Many letters deal with questions of theory and practice, others have to do with family and relationship matters. Upon his father's death, Tom inherited this correspondence and felt an obligation to see it into print. This turned out to be a complex and expensive project. Ann Lammers was hired as editor and translator (with Ursula Egli, a Swiss friend of Tom's who had been his secretary during his IAAP presidency), and considerable funds had to be raised to support this important project. In 2011, the work appeared in a handsome volume published by Routledge.[5] Tom had fulfilled a deeply felt obligation to his father's legacy,

---

[4] Kirsch, Thomas B. (2000). *The Jungians*. New York and London: Routledge.
[5] Lammers, Ann Conrad (Ed.). (2011). *The Jung-Kirsch Letters*. London and New York: Routledge.

and in his later years he lectured widely on the relationship and dialogue between James Kirsch and Jung.

One of the important themes in this correspondence pertained to Jung's attitude toward Jews and Judaism. In 1934 Jung had published what became a notorious statement regarding "Jewish psychology." Many of his Jewish students protested to him personally, notably Erich Neumann. James Kirsch was one of Jung's main defenders against charges of anti-Semitism and pro-Nazi sympathies, while at the same time explaining to Jung the grievous errors he had made in publishing these words and offering to instruct him in the history of Jewish thought, especially in its mystical tradition, the Kabbalah. Tom would later inherit the onerous task of explaining his Jungian identity to Jewish critics, especially to Freudian psychoanalysts. Defending his affiliation with Jung in these settings was one of Tom's most unpleasant tasks in life, and the heated discussions and confrontations at conferences and in professional meetings brought him to a state of extreme anguish on occasion. This was the heavy burden of being a Jewish Jungian in the climate that prevailed after WWII and to a degree continues to this day. Tom carried this burden well and never wavered in his support of his father's position in this matter.

Most people who met Tom and got to know him even casually would speak of his warm personality and his finely tuned extroverted feeling function. I had the good fortune to meet Tom in 1973 at a Jungian conference (it was called the North-South Conference at the time, referring to the meeting of analysts from the San Francisco Bay Area and the Los Angeles area, but had opened to a more national gathering by the time I attended in 1973). Later, we met each other from time to time in various professional contexts, and in 1981, he invited me to join the Program Committee for the next IAAP Congress to be held in Berlin in 1983. Following this, we became close friends through our collaboration on IAAP business. It was always a pleasure to work with Tom, and this continued through his presidency when I served as his Honorary Secretary. The world was opening up to Jungian psychology, and we traveled widely on behalf of the IAAP. There are also many fond memories of our families traveling together in Eastern Europe in 1986 and to China in 1994. In every instance, Tom was open to exploration of new territories and generous in his hospitality to all we came into contact with. He was keen to introduce Jung to the world. I would later come to think of him as "the great pollinator." Not with missionary zeal but with open willingness to assist those who wanted to hear and learn about Jung, Tom traveled the world lecturing, teaching, supervising and generally offering the perspective on the psyche and on life that we know as "Jungian." In 2009 and together with his wife, Jean, Tom travelled to Taiwan to give lectures on Jungian psychology to a new group of students there, and in his later years devoted a great deal of time and energy to developing a strong Jungian presence in Taipei. For many, he was a living symbol of the Jungian attitude and way of life. This was based on more than persona. It was an authentic expression of who he was.

In 2012, Tom was diagnosed with renal cancer and underwent extensive oncological treatment over the course of the following five years. He also developed a case of late onset diabetes in his last years. Despite these serious illnesses, he continued lecturing and teaching worldwide, in Europe, Taiwan and China as well as at home in the United States. In 2016 and shortly before his 80th birthday, he gave the annual June 6 Jung Memorial Lecture in Zurich. The following day I had the pleasure of interviewing him in Jung's library in Kusnacht where he had met Jung and spent an hour with him some 60 years earlier. The film of the interview shows Tom summing up his memories of Zurich and of the early community of Jungians as he experienced them. More about the filmed interview follows.

In addition to his love for Jungian psychology, Tom had a passion for sports and for classical music. He was an avid and skilled tennis player in his younger years and a devoted fan of the San Francisco Giants baseball team to the end of his days. Mozart was perhaps his favorite composer, although he had a broad range of tastes in the classical repertoire all the way from Bach to Mahler. Chamber music was a special love of his, and he would rarely miss the opportunity of attending a concert in Palo Alto or San Francisco.

In 1968, Tom married Jean Kirsch, who also became a well-known Jungian analyst, teacher, and author. They have one child, Susannah (b. 1970), who with her husband, John Kutz, has given them three grandchildren (Hildegard, Jasper, and Theia). By an earlier marriage, Tom had one child, David (b. 1960), who with his wife, Andrea, also gave Tom the blessing of grandchildren (Jacob and Isabel).

INTRODUCTION

Tom died peacefully at his home in Palo Alto, California, on October 22, 2017, attended by his wife and children. Of his four half siblings (Ruth, Michael, James, and Gerald), only Ruth (age 89) is still living.

The Setting of the Interview

At first, it was just a wishful fantasy, then it became a serious plan, and finally it turned into a reality, thanks to the gracious hospitality of Andreas Jung. C.G. Jung's library would be the site of the interview with Tom Kirsch. We were all pleased, not to say excited, to be able to hold and film this historic conversation in a place of such august ambiance.

The library in Jung's house on Seestrasse in Kusnacht, a community on the east side of Lake Zurich, not far to the south of the city of Zurich, has long been a place of fascination for Jung's students and admirers. Here, the famous Swiss psychologist studied his books, met his patients, and sat with his visitors. The windows look out across the garden to Lake Zurich, and on a summer's day you can see sailboats scudding about on the water.

The picture below shows how the library looked in 1909 when Carl, Emma and their three children moved into their new home, just recently completed to house their growing family and Jung's psychoanalytic practice.

This is where Jung welcomed his patients and guests and where he spent many hours in conversation with colleagues and visitors from all over the world. And it is where he kept his famous Red Book during his

How Jung's library looked in 1909.

lifetime. Today this room still houses his library of scholarly works, among them the rare alchemy books he treasured so highly.

As is evident in the photograph of 1909, the room casts an aura of cultural engagement. The three busts of historic figures reveal something about young Carl Jung's cultural heritage. One is left to wonder what influences they may have channeled during the years he carried out his early psychoanalytic researches into mythology and religion that culminated in *Wandlungen und Symbole der Libido* (translated in 1916 as *Psychology of the Unconscious*, revised and retitled forty years later as *Symbols of Transformation*). We see: the sardonically smiling French *philosophe*, Voltaire, set at eye level on the tile Kachelofen to the left of the entrance; the

INTRODUCTION

brilliant German philosopher and bitter critic of Christian culture, Friedrich Nietzsche, standing high up on a bookshelf and overseeing the entire room; and the dignified Roman consul and military hero, Scipio, with his back to a mirror and set down firmly on a sturdy cabinet filled with books. The cultural amalgam represented in his library by this strange trio of figures—French irony and wit, German acidic criticism, and Roman force and strategic thinking—were mixed into Jung's brilliant early writings to create a unique tone of voice and presence. A trained ear can hear their influence between the lines of works like *Wandlungen* and also in the only recently published *The Red Book*, which was begun in this room over 100 years before our visit and the filming of the interview.

Today Jung's library does not look so different from how it would have appeared to a visitor in 1909, thanks to the meticulous preservation efforts carried out by the Stiftung C.G. Jung Kusnacht under the guidance of grandson, Andreas Jung.[6] One noticeable change in the picture below is the absence of the busts, which have been removed and replaced by photographs and a collection of objects, including two skulls in a display of *momento mori*. The famous alchemy collection, put together after Jung's intensive studies in this field began in the early 1930s, now fills the bookshelves just to the right of the entry.

---

[6] The pictures are from *The House of C.G. Jung: The History and Restoration of the Residence of Emma and Carl Gustav Jung-Rauschenbach*, edited by the Stiftung C.G. Jung Kusnacht (Stiftung C.G. Jung Kusnacht, 2009).

Tom and Murray preparing for the interview.

This room would be the setting for my interview with Tom on June 7, 2016, just a few days before his 80th birthday. The plan was to give Tom a chance to talk about, among other things, his meeting with Jung in this room some sixty years earlier.

Even today a *genius loci* seems to inhabit this room, which is, of course, Jung's. It is a challenge to describe the feelings that came to me as we sat in this historic space. I was keenly aware that a hundred years earlier Jung was working here on his Red Book, now published but for years hidden away under lock and key. Many famous personalities from all parts of the world had arrived here to meet the famous psychologist and had spent hours here in deep conversation. It was maybe not quite an occasion for breaking into Mozart's aria, "*in diesen heiligen Hallen*," but something along those lines might passed through the back of our minds as Tom and I sat down together and engaged in con-

INTRODUCTION

versation. We both love Mozart's "Magic Flute," and Tom had written his thesis at the Jung Institute in San Francisco on the symbolism in this magnificent work of art. This setting definitely gave our interview a special feeling tone as though in a sanctuary, or temenos. This emotional tone is better captured in the film than on the page. The camera shows subtle shades of feeling that our words may not convey in print, but even the best camera in the world could not pick up the invisible presence of Jung in this place, on this day.

So many other spirits, too, could be sensed to inhabit the imaginal spaces in this room and out of reach of the cameras: the ancient Gnostics and Church Fathers whom Jung loved and whose works rest upon the shelves; alchemists like Gerhard Dorn and Eleazer the Jew, whose texts are so frequently quoted in Jung's alchemy writings; philosophers like Kant and Schopenhauer, who guided Jung's critical thinking from start to finish; physicians and healers like Paracelsus and C.G. Carus, who directed his intuitions to mysterious depths; above all Goethe, the last of the alchemists by Jung's reckoning, whose Faust occupied his imagination throughout his life; Wagnerian characters like Wotan, Siegfried, Amfortas, Kundry and Parsifal singing faintly in the background. And, of course, Freud, who visited this room in 1909 and discussed psychoanalytic matters here with his favorite pupil, Carl Jung, never faded from the scene entirely and in fact continued to look over Jung's shoulder, even during his late works, such as *Mysterium Coniunctionis* and "Approaching the Unconscious." All of these figures contributed to the atmosphere of this room as we sat down and began our conversation.

Some Background Information about the Making of the Filmed Interview

A great debt of gratitude is owed to Luis Moris and his cameraman, Franck Guillemain, for their efforts in bringing this interview onto the screen. Luis Moris was a part of this work from its conception. This took place shortly after he had completed filming nine interviews with senior analysts at ISAP-Zurich. Hearing about Tom's invitation to Zurich to deliver the annual Jung Memorial Lecture on June 6, 2016, he had the idea to film the lecture and to do an interview with Tom while he was in town. This led to his asking me if I would conduct the interview, and I thought about the possibility of doing it in Jung's library. The film would be historic! What an exciting prospect! Andreas Jung, when asked for permission, proved more than amenable and welcomed the plan, so Luis and Franck set about arranging the logistics for filming while Tom and I began discussing some points of interest to cover in the interview.

Thankfully, the weather was idyllic on June 7 when Tom, his wife, Jean, my wife, Jan, and I arrived at Jung's house at 10:00 o'clock in the morning. Luis and Franck had arrived earlier and were filming the garden and grounds, which would serve as additional background for the film. We then began sketching in the steps to be taken for making this an event to be remembered. The director was Luis, while Tom and I were the actors in this piece of theater. Franck quietly worked with the camera, practically invisible to us as he danced in front, behind, and all around. Andreas was the welcoming host, greeting us as we arrived at the entrance of the house, above which Jung had placed the

INTRODUCTION

famous Delphic oracle, *Vocatus atque non vocatus deus aderit* ("Called or not called, the god is present"). As we stepped into the house, Andreas led us on the way up the winding staircase to the room where Jung would greet his patients and guests. We felt ourselves to be in good hands.

Tom's health at the time of the interview was fragile. As he tells us in the interview, he was in treatment for cancer and suffering from late onset diabetes. He was only days away from his 80th birthday, which was one of reasons this interview would be especially significant for him and for those who appreciate his stature in the Jungian world. He had recently published his autobiographical memoir, *My Life as a Jungian*, which covers his years from his mother's womb to his late 70s. Tom is among the very few Jungian psychoanalysts living today whose parents were also Jungian analysts and who had worked directly with Jung and the first generation of Jungians in Zurich. Tom's earlier book, *The Jungians*, covers the history of the Jungian movement worldwide from its inception to the year 2000. In a sense, Tom's life is synonymous with Jungian history. Now he was in Zurich to deliver the Jung Memorial Lecture for 2016, a year that marked the 55th anniversary of Jung's death. This would presumably be Tom's last visit to Zurich, a city he could claim as his second home, having been here so frequently since his teenage years. All together this was an event to remember and to memorialize in film.

The Interview

In March, 1959, John Freeman interviewed Jung for the BBC in this same room. Freeman was an editor of New Statesman at the time and later became British Ambassador to Washington.[7] Freeman's interview, titled "Face to Face," has become a classic of the genre and according to the editors of *C.G. Jung Speaking* has "undoubtedly brought Jung to more people than any other piece of journalism and any of Jung's own writings."[8] The secret of its success is the comfort level achieved between interviewer and subject. Jung is shown as relaxed and completely open to answering any questions thrown his way. He is altogether natural and comfortable with his interlocutor. This is what I wanted to achieve with Tom, and I believe I was successful.

What I aimed for was to draw Tom into an intimate conversation between friends, such as would take place if we sat in a room at his home in Palo Alto. The fact that we were sitting in Jung's library and were being filmed should slip away and feature only as an interesting background. In the film, it is evident that Tom feels little self-consciousness about the imposing setting or the presence of cameras. We are simply two old friends reminiscing about his history in Zurich and his memories of significant people and events experienced in this birthplace of Jungian psychology.

I wanted the audience to be surprised by Tom's responses to some of my comments and questions, and

---

[7] McGuire, W., & Hull, R.F.C. (Eds.). (1977). *C.G. Jung Speaking*, 424. N.J.: Princeton University Press.
[8] Ibid.

INTRODUCTION

I knew of some topics that would produce this result. The first was about his recollection of having a session with Jung in this room when he was a young man. I knew the story, and I knew the surprise. Tom could recall almost nothing of the interview! He was overwhelmed by emotion to be in the presence of the Great Man! It was as though, if I were in his place and given my early history, I had been granted an hour with Jesus of Nazareth. What could one possibly recall from such a numinous experience? Words and details fail and are lost to the magnetism of the Presence one is confronted with. Tom handles this introductory gambit in the interview with humor and humility. Obviously, he is no longer in the grip of such archetypal transference and now can smile at his earlier state of mind.

A delicate topic was Tom's present state of health and the prospect of dying. This was territory I had not explored in detail with him beforehand, and I was not sure how he would respond. So it came as a relief and something of surprise that he was so completely open to discussing his condition. The interview could then segue into some explorations of spirituality and meaning. Tom reflects on the extension of life given him by the experimental treatments he is receiving for his cancer, and he brings it to the surprising point that this interview is invested with meaning by virtue of this gift. Because he has been granted more time, he makes use of it by contributing to his legacy as a Jungian. I found this moving and continue to feel gratitude that I could be a part of this phase of Tom's life.

Tom and I have been friends and colleagues for over 35 years. We have worked together on numerous committees and projects, we have traveled to many parts of the world together, we have shared the platform at a multitude of conferences, and we have enjoyed meals, music, and wine together. I owe a great deal to Tom since he brought me into the international world of Jungians when he asked me to be his Honorary Secretary while he served as president of the IAAP from 1989 to 1995. I have always found him to be understanding and kind, and in his later years, although our times together have diminished due to geographical distance between our homes since my wife and I moved to Switzerland in 2003, I have found him to be ever more gentle, open and emotionally accessible. In the interview, I think the viewer can see what I mean. There is an unusual transparency in this man. His is humble and he is quietly thoughtful. Above all, he is honest with himself and with us. There is no boasting about his accomplishments, which are considerable, or about the people he has known. There is a kind of simple joy and gratitude. His face shows the beauty of suffering.

As we left Jung's house after the interview, I had the distinct feeling that two souls had met and communicated. Walking down the tree-lined avenue together, we continued the conversation that had begun earlier, and I knew that we would always feel a deep rapport with one another. I can truly say that it has been a great privilege to know Tom for all these years, and now more than ever I appreciate his extraordinary gift of friendship.

INTRODUCTION

A Footnote

Following the interview, Tom continued to struggle with cancer for more than a year, and he continued also to lecture and write although at a slower pace than in earlier times. We were in contact by phone and email from time to time and enjoyed our final conversation just a few days before his death. I look back on the interview as a miraculous moment of opportunity to capture something of Tom's spirit and to do so in a place so significant to us both. Our love of Jung brought us together in the first place, and this is what has held our relationship in place through all the years of a working together.

Jung's house and library became a museum in early 2018 and is open to the public upon request. The bust of Voltaire will once again return to its former place in the library.

Bust of Voltaire.

The Arch of My Life
June 6th Memorial Lecture
by Thomas Kirsch

Den 25th Juni, 1936
Dr. James Kirsch
3 Devonshire Place
London W.1

Lieber Kirsch,
Zu der Geburt Ihres Kindes congratulieze ich Ihnen und Ihrer verehenten Frau Gemahlin aufs herzlichste.
Mit den besten Grussen,
Ihr stets ergebener

That was my first connection to C.G. Jung, analytical psychology, and Zurich. I was born on June 1936 in London. My father, with his new wife, Hilde Silber, a former patient, had arrived in London 10 months previously to begin new lives. They had left Germany in 1933 after Hitler had come to power and had resettled in Palestine. My father had been an ardent Zionist but had been disillusioned by his experience in Palestine. Erich Neumann had arrived in Palestine a few months after my parents, but they did not get along with each other, certainly some sibling rivalry. It may have been a factor in my parents leaving for London. They each had two children from their previous marriages, and I was supposed to be the product of analyzed parents. I was to be the model child. Looking back almost 80 years, I realize that the projection on me was a concretization of what should have been an inner child for each of them. It was early on in Jungian analysis, and the goals for analysis were extremely idealistic. My parents had settled in London with the idea that they would live the rest of their days there. Nazi-ism and Hitler were already very much on the horizon, and there was some question whether it was appropriate to have a child under these conditions. They went ahead with my birth. Jung wrote a short congratulatory note to my father on June 25th on my birth. Nothing else. Both my parents having had analyses with Jung, I was to be the fruit of successful analyses.

When World War II began in 1939, it looked as if Great Britain would succumb to the forces of the Wehrmacht, and that all of Europe, including Great Britain, would be under Nazi domination. My father, having been born in Guatemala, was able to obtain affidavits for his family to enter the United States, as well as tickets on the Cunard liner the Samaria. The German and U.K. quotas were oversubscribed, and it would have been difficult to find passage. It was an extremely dangerous crossing in September-October 1940 at a time when the Nazi U-boats were sinking 350,000 tons of British ships every month. We had a large convoy and luckily made it to New York. I was interviewed by a New York newspaper, because it was unusual for a ship to make it across the North Atlantic.

THE ARCH OF MY LIFE

Photos of Samaria and PASSENGER LIST

My father visited his uncles in San Francisco, and on the way back to New York went to Los Angeles where a large German-Jewish refugee population had settled. It reminded him of Guatemala and Tel Aviv and he brought the family to Los Angeles by the end of 1940. My parents immediately began to develop a Jungian community, and six months later they were joined by Max and Lore Zeller.

Almost immediately, my father began to give evening seminars, at first mainly on untranslated works of Jung, which he continued until the end of 1988. Meanwhile, my mother developed a large analytic practice and later in her life she gave a seminar on Jung's Zarathustra seminar. So, the spreading of Jung's writings and doing analysis became the overriding interest father, and parenting was done mainly by my mother. It was wartime so that there was no actual contact between Jung and my parents after 1941. In a letter to my mother in 1941, Jung had been critical of my parents moving to the United States. He felt their moving from country to country was a sign of restlessness, and they should have remained in London.

My mother frequently asked me about my dreams, and naturally I told them to her. I was fascinated by what she could make of them and her insights. Only later in my own analysis did I realize that there was a level of intrusiveness along with her insights. At her death, she left me a letter which described a dream I had as a young boy where I was swallowed up by the moon. She felt this was a very important message to me. I took this message to my analyst, Joe Henderson, and we talked about the meaning of being swallowed up by the moon. My mother was rightly concerned with my ego being overpowered by the mother archetype, represented by the moon.

I also found my father's weekly evening seminars intrusive to my boyhood interests, but I tolerated them easier than my siblings who developed a negative attitude towards Jung whom they had never met. I found my dreams fascinating and I followed them on a sporadic level, while most of my energy was directed towards adapting to the American way of life, which differed so much from my parent's German Jewish background. I was sent to Hebrew school and continued that for eight years, including a couple of years after my bar mitzvah.

My next significant Jungian contact came at age 14 or 15. I had developed a strong interest in playing tennis, and after school and on weekends I spent several hours going to the neighborhood tennis courts. In Southern California, there was little rain, so that one could play outdoors year-round. My parents were concerned about the amount of time that I devoted to tennis and not to my studies. I was a good student, but both parents thought I should be reading more of the classics and spending less time on sports. As a consequence, my mother sent my horoscope to Ernst Bernhard in Rome for his opinion. They had known him in Berlin as he was a cousin of their friend Max Zeller. He, too, had analyzed with Jung. He had wanted to emigrate to Great Britain, but he was turned away because of his interest in astrology. Instead, he went to Italy where he was placed under house arrest during World War II, but upon the liberation of Rome in 1944, he became the first Jungian analyst in Italy. He analyzed my horoscope and replied to my parents that they should not worry about me. My interest in athletics was natural, and that I would become more interested in academics later on in my life. I think my parents were concerned that I would not become a Jungian analyst, and that is why they contacted Bernhard.

Hilde Kirsch with Ernst Bernhardt.

My parents wanted the family to spend my junior year in high school in Zurich. I was deeply enmeshed in my athletic and social life and made it clear that I did not want to do that and spend a year in Zurich. They realized how important it was not to interrupt my high school experience. So, it did not happen. What they did instead was to each go separately at different times to Zurich to see Jung and to continue their analysis with CA Meier.

By this time, there was a group of at least 50 people in Los Angeles interested in Jungian psychology, and through my parents, they began a fund in order to invite and host prominent analysts from Zurich and London. Thus, I met Marlus von Franz, Rivkah Schaerf Kluger, Gerhard Adler, and Michael Fordham. When a foreign analyst was in town, life took on an excitement and an intensity that was quite remarkable.

It was decided that as a graduation present from high school, my father and I would go to Europe and eventually meet up with my mother in Zurich. This was a life-changing experience because it reconnected me to my European roots, which I had denied growing up in Los Angeles. I have never lost that connection. This was 1953 and the ravages of World War II were still very much in evidence in both Great Britain and France, which my father and I visited before connecting with my mother in Zurich. Arriving in Zurich in 1953 was an amazing experience. After having experienced war-torn England and France, Switzerland seemed like paradise. Everything worked and was on time, and there was no evidence of destruction. On Sunday morning, one heard many church bells for none of the churches had been destroyed. I met my parent's friends, Meier, Liliane Frey, Aniela Jaffe, the Hurwitz family, von Franz and Barbara Hannah, and probably others who I cannot remember at this time. My mother wanted me to have an hour with Meier with the idea that I might start analysis with him. We had a pleasant hour, but he suggested that I should let my neuroses grow, and come back when they are more fully developed. We had a good laugh about that. I especially was attracted to the Hurwitz family because they were Jewish, the two children Immanuel and Naomi were about my age, and they were both very interesting people with talents in music and art. I was quite taken with their sense of family which I idealized. My parents did not practice any Jewish rituals at home, whereas the Hurwitz family had definite Jewish rituals like a Friday night Shabbat dinner.

I returned to the United States and entered my college years with a new sense of purpose. I had read *"Modern Man in Search of a Soul,"* and I thought consciously for the first time that I would become a Jungian analyst. At that time in the United States, it was important to have a medical degree to become any kind of analyst, so I chose a pre-medical major. At the time there was still a Jewish quota at the private medical schools, and I realized that I had to do well academically in order to get into medical school. Jung was considered extremely marginal in those days and none of the Los Angeles Jungian analysts had the proper credentials as far as the collective was concerned. I was being groomed to obtain all the proper credentials, then return to Los Angeles and lead the professional Jungians there.

In February, 1955, much to my surprise and delight, Jung's face appeared on the cover of Time Magazine. At that time, Time Magazine was one of two major news outlets, and so it was a big deal that Jung was on its cover with a long article about him and his psychology. In the spring of 1956, my parents came to visit me at college, and my father offered to give an introductory lecture on Jung. Much to my surprise there was a packed audience, including many of my professors, and my father gave an excellent lecture. This changed my attitude towards him. I began to respect his intellectual capacities, and forgave him for many of the psychological wounds that had occurred between the two of us.

In the summer of 1955, three students and I decided that we would travel together in Europe; one was a classmate from Reed, and two were friends from high school. One of them, an introverted brilliant contemporary during high school, had developed a strong relationship to my father, who had given him all of Jung's books in English to read. Just six weeks before we were to leave for Europe, this friend died lying on his day bed in his dormitory. It was unclear whether the death was accidental or suicide. Later it was determined that it was suicide. The three of us decided to continue as we had already made extensive plans. We stayed with my uncle and aunt in London, where I developed severe abdominal symptoms which most likely was appendicitis. I attempted to see a physician through the newly formed national British health service. But it would have required a six-week waiting time. We called my mother who was in Zurich. She arranged a flight to Zurich and my hospitalization where I had my appendix taken out the next day. My two friends went on to Paris and we were going to meet in Rome after my surgery. That year, 1955, there was a public celebration of Jung's 80th birthday at the Grand Dolder hotel. My mother took me to the reception and pushed me into the receiving line to meet Jung. When she introduced me, I had the impression that he was pleased that I was there. The handshake is what I remember most. It was a warm and almost electric handshake! For many years I thought it was completely transference. However, in 2010 at the Library of Congress, one of Jung's grandchildren mentioned that a handshake with his grandfather was what he remembers most about him. I felt affirmed in my impression of Jung.

The next summer, 1956, my parents again went to Zurich, for my mother was a delegate from Los Angeles to the newly formed IAAP. This gave my father a chance to visit Jung and express his condolences for the death of Emma Jung the previous November. I was invited to go along with him for an afternoon tea. That year, "Two Essays on Analytical Psychology" had been published in

English and in paperback, and I had already read it. I found a statement "all knowledge is relative" so I asked Jung about it. I said it seemed to me that this was an absolute statement, and was that not contradictory? I cannot remember how Jung responded, but maybe he was amused. Since then I have taught "Two Essays" many times, and I have not been able to find that statement ever again. It must have come somewhere from my unconscious.

In June, 1957, I graduated from college, and in that fall I was heading for medical school at the Albert Einstein College of Medicine in New York. I was feeling a number of pressures upon me and thought it might be time to begin analysis. I arranged to come to Zurich and begin with CA Meier on a three-times-a-week basis during that summer. I lived in the service quarters of the Hotel Sonnenberg for less than five dollars a day with all meals. This gave me a lot of time for introversion as well as playing tennis. Meier suggested that I read Kant's *Critique of Pure Reason* to improve my inferior thinking function. I dutifully read the book and enjoyed it very much. Meanwhile, I came to know some of the students at the Jung Institute, such as David Hart, Jim Hillman, Bob Stein, and Marvin Spiegelman. I began to play tennis with them on a regular basis and heard a lot of the gossip going around the Institute. I also audited the course on the Puer Aeternus by Marlus von Franz. In those days it was much easier to audit a class than it is today. At the end of the summer, I joined Lena Hurwitz and her two children for a camping trip in and around Florence, Italy. At the time, neither of them spoke

Top left: Liliane Frey-Rohn; top right, C. A. Meier;
bottom left, Aniela Jaffé; bottom right: Sigmund Hurwitz.

English, and my German improved markedly on that trip. It was a very enjoyable experience.

New York City and Albert Einstein College of Medicine really did not agree with me, and I needed more analysis. I arranged to go back to Zurich for the summer of 1958 and to continue analysis with CA Meier. I saw Liliane Frey when Meier was away on vacation. My father was also in Zurich that summer, both in analysis with Meier and teaching at the Jung Institute. We lived together in a small apartment around the corner from Meier's office, but we had separate lives. Aniela Jaffe telephoned to say that Jung could see my father on a Friday morning, but my father could not make it because he was teaching at the Institute. He asked Aniela whether I could have the appointment instead, and she called back saying that Jung would be delighted to see me. This began a series of conversations with Meier about what I should talk about with Jung. He mentioned my dreams about intersecting circles which he thought would interest Jung. At the time, Jung was working on "Flying Saucers: A Modern Myth of Things Seen in the Sky." When I entered Jung's study, the first thing he said to me was, "So you want to see the old man before he dies." That completely undid me and I honestly cannot remember what we talked about for the rest of the hour. I believe that I did tell him the dreams which I had prepared to discuss, but I cannot remember a specific comment that he made after that beginning. His directness and charisma affected me deeply, and I believe that is when I decided definitively that I would become a Jungian analyst. I also had no idea that Meier and Jung were not speaking to each other socially but only professionally. I learned about that much later from the movie, "Matter of Heart." Later that summer, the first IAAP Congress was held in Zurich. Meier strongly suggested that I not be in Zurich during the Congress, and so I went to London. After my return and after the Congress, my parents and I had dinner with Von Franz and Hannah who could not understand why Jung was so friendly to Fordham whose theories and practices seemed at odds with Jung's. That puzzled me, but subsequently I have realized that Jung valued both the clinical and the symbolic nature of the psyche, and he wanted to make sure that the clinical was given equal value.

I had transferred to Yale Medical School which was much more suitable for me, and there met my first wife who was also a medical student in my class, and we married in June, 1960. She was French Jewish and had been hidden from the Nazis in southern France during World War II. My parents, as a wedding present, gave us a trip to Europe. That trip brought up many unresolved issues between us, and we headed for Zurich. This time both of us saw Meier for a month! That permitted us to continue our journey, but the issues that had come up between us never were completely resolved, and we divorced seven years later. We do have a lovely son, David Kirsch, who is professor of entrepreneurship at the University of Maryland. He and his wife, Andrea, are the proud parents of almost 17-year-old twins, Jacob and Isabel. They will join us later in Zurich and the Engadine. They are approximately the same age I was when I first visited Zurich and the Alps. How the world has changed in the intervening 63 years!

I began my psychiatric residency at Stanford in 1962 and I became a candidate at the San Francisco Jung Institute in the fall of 1963. For the first time, I was in a regular analysis with an analyst who was not also the analyst of my parents or who did not have a negative feeling towards them. Joe Henderson became my primary analyst, teacher, colleague, and friend until his death in 2007 at the age of 104. My primary allegiance shifted to San Francisco, and my earlier connections to Zurich and Los Angeles were transformed in the process.

By 1969, I had remarried to Jean, who had never been to Europe before, and I wanted to introduce her to those people who had been important to me in Zurich, like Meier, Frey, the Hurwitz family, and Aniela Jaffe. I had been certified to be a Jungian analyst in December, 1968. It was an extremely successful visit, and we have been coming back regularly since then.

As much as I love visiting Zurich and the numerous friends that I have made over the years, I have never lived here.

Upon two occasions I could have moved here. The first was when I was applying to medical school, and I thought very seriously of doing it here in Zurich. In the 1950s there was still a quota system against Jews in most American medical schools. Therefore, many Jewish students went to foreign medical schools. Zurich has/had an excellent medical school, but one needed to know German. Sigi Hurwitz saw most of the American Jewish students as their dentist, so he had frequent contact with them. The problem for me was the stigma against these foreign-trained physicians. Since I had gained admission to several U.S. medical schools, I thought it best to study in America so I would not have that stigma with me for the rest of my professional life.

A second opportunity occurred in 1973. Professor C.A. Meier was retiring at the ETH, and was looking for someone to take over his professorship. I had been very interested in rapid eye movement research, also a strong interest of Meier's. He asked me if I would be interested in the position, but it came at a time when I had established myself in Palo Alto. Jean was ready to move to Zurich, but as much as I have enjoyed visiting Zurich, I chose to stay in Palo Alto. Moving to Zurich in 1973 would have been a major midlife life transition. Interestingly enough, that position has never again been fulfilled by a Jungian analyst or scholar.

At my first IAAP Congress in London in 1971, I was nominated by Jo Wheelwright and Jim Hillman to be second vice president. They had not told me that they were going to nominate me, so it came as a complete surprise. I lost by one vote, but this put me in a good position at the next election in 1977 in Rome to become a vice president, and eventually I became president of the IAAP. I was again nominated by Jo Wheelwright, and although Swiss law does not require a second, I did receive one by CA Meier. Adolf Guggenbühl became the president and Jim Hillman was his honorary secretary. Because Hillman and Meier had had a huge rift between them, I was severely criticized by Jim for still being on speaking terms with Meier. What a way to begin!

Over the next 18 years, a new phase grew in my relationship to Jung, analytical psychology, and Zurich. The Guggenbühl's invited me to stay at their house when I came to Zurich for IAAP meetings. I developed relationships with Adolf, Toni Frei, Mario Jacoby, and Sonja Marjaesch. I also maintained a relationship with many of the first generation of Jungians. For the last 12 years of my vice presidency and presidency of the IAAP, I came to Zurich at least twice and sometimes three times a year. I traveled both alone or with family and we would usually stay with the Guggenbühl's. The topics of conversation were numerous and ranged from psychology and philosophy to the politics of the Jungian movement and more personal family matters. I also arranged for the representatives to stay at the Hotel Florhof, before it was remodeled under new ownership to become a much more luxurious place. Zurich truly was a second home to me during those 12 years when I became familiar with different aspects of Zurich culture. My presidency culminated in the 1995 international Congress's return to Zurich where the first congresses had been held, beginning in 1958. The IAAP had grown from around 100 members in 1958 to close to 2,500 members in 1995. Being in Zurich as much as the work for the IAAP required, I came to know my contemporaries here such as Paul Brutsche, Murray Stein, Bob Hinshaw, Luigi Zoya, Peter Amman, Ruth Amman, Sonja Marjaesh, and many others. The combination of being in Zurich and being vice president and president of the IAAP was the richest experience of my professional life.

One painful experience involved the Klinik am Zurichberg where there was a big struggle between Professor C.A. Meier and the psychologist Toni Frei. There was a conflict about who would become the new medical director after Heinrich Fierz. The board was split. I wrote up the struggle in my book "The Jungians" and I listened to Meier's interpretation of events more than Toni's. I still had a lingering transference to Meier, which I only understood after the Klinic experience. Toni was very hurt by my characterization of events at the Klinic when he read that part in my book. I tried to rectify things between us, but it never worked out. By the time I approached him he was already quite ill and was not open to try to work out our friendship. I have always regretted this incident greatly.

The IAAP was in a state of rapid growth when I became president in 1989. Until then it had been primarily a European organization with several American Jungian societies. During my presidency, the Berlin wall fell, and the rest of the world seemed to open up to analytical psychology. A big issue was how to respond to the many requests that we were receiving from all over the world to learn more about Jung and analytical psychology. They came from Eastern Europe, the Soviet Union, much of Latin America, and Asia. When I had begun my analysis in San Francisco in 1962, I was quite a missionary for Jung and analytical psychology. I wanted all my friends and colleagues to get into Jungian analysis. By 1989, when I had become president, I had backed off considerably from my previous attitude. I no longer felt the need to go out and be a missionary for Jung. My connection to Jung and analytical psychology had deepened and had become more inward. I had experienced the shadow of my missionary zeal. This came out most clearly when I visited the Soviet Union and later Russia. From that perspective, I could see that every school of psychotherapy was sending representatives to sell the newly forming psychotherapy community on their particular brand of therapy. I was able to see that very few if any of those initial students would actually want to become Jungian analysts. Exposing the psychotherapy community to Jung's ideas was an important initial step, regardless of whether any of them actually became Jungian analysts. We also tried to make an official Russian translation of the Collected

Works, but we were only able to publish one volume, volume 15, before the Russian politics stopped any further official translations. There are many translations of Jung's work into Russian, but none of them are authorized. Even our translation would've been from the English and not from the German original.

The question remains of how much missionary zeal should the IAAP exert, and how much should the IAAP respond to requests from afar for Jungian analysis and training? That remains a controversial topic which evokes strong emotion for and against... From my point of view, I did a lot of travel as IAAP president, and I see that every administration since has continued with the same tendency to travel extensively. This is because the demand for Jungian ideas remains strong throughout the world. At present, Asia seems to be the fastest growing area of interest in analytical psychology. What would Jung have liked? I believe he would have liked people reading and understanding more about the unconscious. He felt that not many people really understood him, the unconscious, and his ideas about it. I think that is still true today.

In conclusion, Jung as an image and reality has been an ever changing one for me. In my early life, he was a distant and important image, because he was clearly the most important person outside of the immediate family. That affected all of us children in different ways. Through my mother especially, I found great value in my dreams. The next phase was meeting first-generation Jungians in Zurich as a teenager. These colleagues of my parents intrigued me greatly, and I was attracted to the field of analytical psychology. Then I had

THE ARCH OF MY LIFE

Joe Henderson

a need for analysis and saw a Jungian in Zurich and luckily had a chance to meet Jung in person. That was life-changing! After being tempted to study and train in Zurich, I returned to the United States and did my major analysis and training in San Francisco. That was another life-changing transition. Early in my analysis in San Francisco, I had dreams with the image of Jung. These dreams helped me to separate from my identification with Jung the person, and that he gradually become more of a symbol of finding one's own individual way, which for me has been extroverted and feeling intuitive. I was not an introverted thinking intuitive type like Jung, which my parents wanted me to be. This brought me into the international political and administrative world of analytical psychology, and that suited me very well. I continued to have a relationship with Joe Henderson until his death at 104, which helped me to keep contact with my introverted side while I was living out this extroverted side. My wife has also been an important influence on keeping me grounded. So, Jung has been in my life from the very beginning until now. The image of Jung continues to evolve in my psyche. It has been a great honor to share my Jungian life with you.

Thomas B. Kirsch in Conversation with Murray Stein in the Home of C.G. Jung

by **Thomas B. Kirsch and Murray Stein**

The Setting: This interview took place in the library of C.G. Jung's home at 228 Seestrasse, Kusnacht, Switzerland. It is the room that houses Jung's collection of alchemy books and was the location of his work on *The Red Book*. In 2017, this space will become part of a museum and open to the public.
The Date: June 8, 2016.

Murray: Tom, you are going to be 80 years old in few days.
Tom: Right.
Murray: Congratulations!
Tom: Thank you! Thank you very much!
Murray: And you were here in this very room some 58 years ago.
Tom: Yes. That's correct.
Murray: When you were 22 years old.
Tom: That's right.
Murray: How does it feel to be here? Is it the same room, does it look the same as it did then?

Tom: Actually, I have no memory of how the room looked when I was 22.
Murray: You didn't see it? You were in this room and you didn't see it?
Tom: No! I mean, this is the kind of thing that Jean, my wife, gets upset with me about because I do not register sensate details. I am not a sensation type, and I just do not take in details like that. What I took in was Jung standing over me and inviting me to sit down and saying: "So you want to see the old man before he dies!" I remember him just knocking me over. At that point, I was overwhelmed.
Murray: Did you speak English with him?
Tom: Oh yes, of course. In one of the letters in the correspondence with my father, he said that after World War II he spoke more English than anything else.
Murray: Really? I'm surprised.
Tom: Yes, really! I mean, whatever the English part of his practice was, he spoke more English than any other language.
Murray: He was very comfortable in English, it seems.
Tom: Oh, yes. He had a thick Swiss accent, the Basler accent, as Paul Brutsche has demonstrated so well in his performances of Jung, but his English was otherwise perfect.
He had a large vocabulary in English.
Murray: Your father must have come here to this room many times, right?
Tom: Oh, yes.
Murray: He was in analysis with Jung, right?
Tom: He had over 60 hours of analysis with Jung, which in those days was considered a lot of hours. He started the analysis in 1929. Because so many of Jung's patients

THOMAS B. KIRSCH IN CONVERSATION WITH MURRAY STEIN IN THE HOME OF C.G. JUNG

A Party at the C.G. Jung Institute in Zurich, 1954.

were not from Zurich, they would come for a period of time, maybe for some weeks or a few months, and then leave and later return to see him again. 60 hours of analysis with Jung was considered a lot at the time, but it was broken up.

Murray: So, a tough question: How are you different from your father?

Tom: Oh, my God! Well, there are many ways that we are different. He was really a scholar and he read a voluminous amount of material.

Murray: Heavy, serious material, I suppose.

Tom: Oh yes, serious material. When he died, I cannot remember how many books I had to go through that he had. He had books in French, English, German, and Hebrew, and I ended up giving the Hebrew books to the Hebrew University in Los Angeles. The French and a lot of the German books I gave to Adolf Guggenbühl. I kept about 10 percent of the English books, many of which I already had, some from him. It took a week to go through his books, a whole week, so it was quite a tour, because I could not do it very long at a time. I would go through books, and I would have associations to the material and would have to stop.

Murray: I know you are not that kind of a scholar, but on the other hand you have written lot of papers and several books. Still, you don't have that kind of interest in alchemy and philosophy and so forth, which your father had in such abundance.

Tom: I have read some alchemy, but my father, for instance, made 600 audiotapes on Jung's "Psychology of the Transference" and *Mysterium Coniunctionis*. There was an expectation that I would follow in doing that and take up where he left off.

Murray: That's my next question. You are burdened with a destiny in a way, or set up, as you say, "to go into the family business."

Tom: Yes, I like calling it that. It de-potentiates the whole thing a bit.

Murray: Of course, but do you also have the feeling that it was somehow destined? Now looking back from vantage point of 80 years, do you see that there was a meaning to this destiny? You have contributed so much to analytical psychology; your whole life has been in a sense dedicated to it. Is there a personal, but also beyond that, do you think there is also a kind of synchronistic meaning to it? I mean, to the timing of your involvement in the Jungian movement, if we can call it that, globally?

Tom: Well... I think there is. But let me take a roundabout way to answer you. I was diagnosed with kidney cancer four and a half years ago. I had a partial removal

THOMAS B. KIRSCH IN CONVERSATION WITH MURRAY STEIN IN THE HOME OF C.G. JUNG

of one kidney, and they found out a very few months later that I had metastasis to the lungs. And so, I thought to myself: I am not going to live very much longer. I was at the Stanford University Hospital, which is an outstanding medical center, one of the best in the whole world. They put me on some medications, which worked for a while but then stopped being effective. So, my metastasis started getting larger. I thought, oh, that's the end. But then they put me on a study. The study was to test a new medication, a whole new approach to cancer, which is to enhance the immune system and then the immune system selectively kills off the cancer cells. There are four drugs now that have been approved for that kind of treatment. So, I was put on the study of that, and that was two and a half years ago, and I have improved since then. The nodules in my lungs are either the same size or smaller, but no new ones have appeared. I bring this up because I think: Why I am still alive? I am going to turn 80 soon, now I am here in Zurich, and there must be something still for me to do. I look on this interview as one of those things. Because I realize that at this point, there are not many people still alive who knew Jung, and I also knew a lot of the early people who are very significant in the Jungian movement. My first analyst was the crown prince to Jung... certainly, a bad thing to be a crown prince, not an enviable position to have.

Murray: No, usually you're knocked off the step to the throne before you reach the goal.

Tom: Yes, you get knocked off.

Murray: Back to your illness, Tom. How has it changed your life? You are carrying a heavy burden, and you have to have frequent treatments. Has this changed you significantly?

Tom: I have had less interest to do a lot of traveling and giving of seminars, and I have been far more selective. I know that whatever I do take on, I really want to or I won't do it. And when I say no, I know I'll never be asked again. So, it's a kind of slowdown, a kind of withdrawal of energy from being so active in the professional world.

Murray: But you are still active. You came to Zurich!

Tom: I couldn't turn that down!

Murray: Why?

Tom: Because it was the anniversary of Jung's death. I was here, as you were, at the 50th anniversary, and I found that a very significant event.

Murray: Yes. Your father's correspondence with Jung was published at just that time.

Tom: Yes, and I love Zurich anyway. So, I mean, bringing everything together, it was a natural thing to do for me, I did not have to think about it. I did not have to throw an I Ching or have a dream about it or anything like that. I just said "yes."

Murray: Yes, the combination of things would be pretty hard to resist. There is a tradition in Zurich, as you know, of holding a special lecture on June 6th every year to commemorate Jung's death in 1961. This year you were invited to give this lecture. This event is sponsored by three institutions here in Switzerland: the Swiss Society of Analytical Psychology, the Jung Institute in Kusnacht, and the International School of Analytical Psychology in Zurich. Plus, it's your 80th birthday, and this may be your last trip to Zurich, though you don't know.

Tom: I don't know.

THOMAS B. KIRSCH IN CONVERSATION WITH MURRAY STEIN IN THE HOME OF C.G. JUNG

Murray: We hope not.
Tom: I hope not too, but if I take any more trips across the water, across any large body of water, it would be here.
Murray: In a sense, Zurich is your second home. It is like a spiritual home.
Tom: Oh, yes, it is. I have spent a lot of time here, even though I have never lived here. I did spend two entire summers here, though. I came here a lot.
Murray: So, it feels very familiar to you.
Tom: It's very familiar.
Murray: It's 55 years since Jung died. And it's, I think, 60 years since the International, the IAAP, was founded.
Tom: Actually, I have the picture of when they were sitting up in the Sonnenberg and drafting the idea for an International Association. That was the meeting where they were gathering together for first time as delegates from the different societies that existed at that time in 1955. A year later the IAAP was actually founded and a first president elected.
Murray: Since the IAAP had its headquarters here in Zurich, that was reason for you to come here so often when you were on the Executive Committee and then later president, a total of 15 years, I believe. I well remember when you as President asked me to be your Honorary Secretary. I was so thrilled, and we had a wonderful time running the Executive Committee in those years from 1989-1995. I remember that the license plates on your car read: "IAAP"!
Tom: Oh, I did that! You can do that in California if you can pay 25 dollars extra for your license plate. You can

put whatever you want on there, within reason of course.

Murray: I know the IAAP was very special to you. It really became the center of your life for a number of years.

Tom: Yes.

Murray: Can you say something about that? What did the IAAP mean to you? You were rooted in California, had a successful analytic practice, lots of teaching and so on. To pull yourself away from all of that, to some extent at least, and engage with the international scene must have meant a sacrifice.

Tom: I did not know that the IAAP was going to become so important to me. As I said in the lecture at ISAP last night, I was first nominated for the position of second vice president without people telling me that they were going to nominate me. As a matter of fact, I was not even supposed to be a delegate from San Francisco to that Congress in Rome because I was a new member. Some of the older members who were not made delegates were pretty upset. James Hillman and Jo Wheelwright had been working behind the scenes without telling me. Once in the Executive Committee, I got "the bug," and it fit me because I have natural extraversion, which is still there, and I'm a feeling type, so that works very well. It's not the only good typology for the job—you are a very good organizer and you have been a very good President too—but it fit for me and it fit for the organization at that time.

Murray: Yes, you did fit the need of the times very well, and that's why I used the term synchronicity a while back, because the timing was extraordinary. You became IAAP president in 1989, just at the end of the Cold War, and the world was opening up for the first time in our lifetimes.

Tom: Oh, it was an amazing job to have at an amazing time.

Murray: And you did such a good job of extending Jungian work into those new parts of the world.

Tom: Having been so much a missionary for Jung earlier in my life and then to have that ... well, I had had a lot of analysis about what Jung meant for me. Because of meeting him personally, and then four years later beginning an analysis with Joe Henderson, and starting psychiatry and telling my professors that I have just met Jung ... it was a little weird.

Murray: I would certainly think so.

Tom: I had trouble because of that—there was envy. They did not know what to do with me. Jung was in some sense very famous, but on the other hand he was marginal. Everything was Freud and psychoanalysis at that time, and so it was not an easy place to be. Also, the fact that I am Jewish and there were questions about Jung and anti-Semitism and all that.... So, I had to answer a lot of questions. I have had to play a lot of roles in my time.

Murray: But while it was difficult for you personally, to have a president of the IAAP who is Jewish going around the world speaking about Jung, I think did do quite a bit to push back, or at least to allay, the accusations that he was an anti-Semite and a Nazi. But you took a quite lot of abuse.

Tom: Definitely, I got a lot of abuse in that role, I really did.

Murray: I know some conferences you went to were very difficult.

Tom: Yes, there was one such conference in particular. It was sponsored by The International Association for the Study of the History of Psychoanalysis, and it was held in Versailles in the year 2000. The IAAP put some money into it, and I was on a panel. My 20-minute talk was on Jung as Freud's first critic, and I talked about some of the things that Jung disagreed with—you know, that not everything is sexual, the different approach to dreams and some other things. I presented this as if as today, in the year 2000, this would be acceptable and people would not protest too strongly. I finished my talk, and I got couple of cursory comments, and then one woman from New York whom I had never met before nor since got up and said: "There is an elephant in the room!" And then she went on to say that there are people in this room whose relatives were indirectly killed by Jung because he supported Nazis, and that he supported the concentration camps, etcetera. There was a silence in the room, tension. . . .

Murray: I can imagine!

Tom: . . . . and I kind of lost it. I was really upset because there were people like Otto Kernberg in the audience. It was, you know, a high-level psychoanalytic audience. I ended up by saying that my mother and father were both in analysis with Jung in the '30s, when he was supposed to have been most anti-Semitic and most connected to the Nazis, and they both felt that he wasn't at all anti-Semitic or pro-Nazi. My mother had been a secularized Jew, and she didn't even know what it meant to be Jewish, really, until Hitler came on the scene and when that whole business started in late '20s. My father had been raised an Orthodox Jew and found his family very materialistic and had rejected Orthodox Judaism. Jung became his spiritual father. So, I started talking about that, and people got on me afterwards and said: "You can't use that kind of personal story to get Jung off the hook." But that's what I did, and I got completely emotional. After the initial criticism for having gotten so emotional, actually I was glad I let it hit me rather than just giving some kind of intellectual answer and quoting some books and articles by other people.

Murray: Had you not faced this kind of a challenge earlier as well? I mean, growing up in Los Angeles, your father being a Jungian analyst in the very strong psychoanalytic immigrant community there, there must have been a lot of criticism of Jung.

Tom: There was a lot of criticism. My father was in a study group in the clinical setting of the Cedars Lebanon Hospital, Los Angeles, which included the well-known psychoanalytic writer, Otto Fenichel. Fenichel was doing an internship at the time so he could get licensed as a physician in California, and in the middle of it he died of a heart attack. He was in his mid-40s. My dad was going to do the same thing and he never did, because after that, he thought, if it killed Fenichel, it could kill me, too. So, he never could practice in California as a doctor, he could never utilize the MD that he got from a very reputable university in Germany, Heidelberg. He actually was sued a couple of times because he didn't have the proper license. If my dad spoke anywhere, and there were psychoanalysts in the audience, they would actually get up and leave. It was very tense in those days. An interesting thing was that there were couples in which one would see a Freudian psychoanalyst, the other one see either my mother or father, so the analysts had to talk at times. When I was a resident at Stanford, I presented a case to Leo Rangell. He was 60 at the time and a very famous psychoanalyst—he had been president of the IPA and had written God-knows-how-many books and articles. So, when one of the professors said, "Oh, do you know who is presenting? This is Tom Kirsch, the son of James and Hilda Kirsch," he replied: "Oh, I know them." It was like that.

Murray: You went to Albert Einstein University in New York to study medicine. How was that experience?

Tom: Well, that that was different. First of all, I went to Albert Einstein because my father had two friends from medical school who had an influence on us. One was Erich Fromm, with whom he remained lifelong friends. Fromm was probably the only psychoanalyst that he counted as a friend, really till Fromm's death. The other was a man named Ernst Simon who went to Israel and became kind of a colleague and collaborator with Martin Buber. He had come to spend a sabbatical year in Los Angeles when I was in college. My mother really liked him, and so I became friends with him, too. He became kind of a mentor for me. I decided to go to Einstein because I thought I should go to a Jewish medical school. The teacher I had at Einstein was a woman name Sibylle Escalona, and she was a colleague of Bruno Klopfer, the person who most promoted the Rorschach Test in the United States. She was very nice to me. He wrote to her and said I was coming. We read

THOMAS B. KIRSCH IN CONVERSATION WITH MURRAY STEIN IN THE HOME OF C.G. JUNG

Erikson's *Childhood and Society*—that was the assignment for a first-year medical student. It was very good.

Murray: Did you ever meet Erikson?

Tom: Yes, I did. He lived in the Bay Area for a while, but he had to leave in the 1950s. At the height of McCarthyism in the early '50s, all the people at the University of California, which is where he was teaching, had to sign a loyalty oath. He refused, he wouldn't do it, and so he lost his tenured professorship at CAL. That's when he went to Harvard. But in those many years that he was at CAL, one of his very best friends was Jo Wheelwright. He and Jo Wheelwright were just as close as could be. I went to several parties at Jo's where I saw Erikson and could talk with him. At Jo and Jane Wheelwright's 50th wedding anniversary, the Erikson's were there. It was a small group of maybe 20 or 30 people.

Murray: You mentioned Jo Wheelwright in your anniversary lecture, and you mentioned Joe Henderson as well. In fact, dedicated your talk to your friend and analyst, Joe Henderson. We'll come back to him in a bit. What about Wheelwright? He claimed to be the only Jungian extrovert in the world.

Tom: Jo Wheelwright was the only Jungian in the States who had an academic position in his time. He was a professor of psychiatry at Langley-Porter, and he hobnobbed mainly with psychoanalysts. He was criticized by the Jungians for doing that, but in retrospect I can see that was really a very natural thing for him to do. This was in the '40s and the '50s, when there was tremendous tension between the Freudians and the Jungians. There were people around who had analyzed with Freud, like Roy Grinker in Chicago, and people who had analyzed with Jung, so the tension was very personal.

Murray: In San Francisco for a quite a long time, only medical people could train as Jungian analysts, isn't that right? It was structured along Freudian lines in that sense.

Tom: In the beginning, during the first three or four years from 1940 to 1944, there were only MDs who practiced as Jungian analysts. The psychologists then protested vehemently, and they formed their own separate non-medical society of Jungian analysts. These were people like Kate Broadway and Claire Thompson; and then very shortly thereafter they all got together and formed the Society of Jungian Analysts of Northern California. For the next 10 or 15 years, you could be either an MD or a psychologist and get equal treatment. Then there was another group who started wanting to be trained, and that was a group with a master's degree in Social Work and Marriage and Family Therapy. So eventually the barriers got broken down, and at this point we have as many social worker analysts as we do psychologists and psychiatrists.

Murray: Do you think anything was lost by this, or gained? What's your opinion?

Tom: You know, it is like so many things in life. It was both a loss and a gain. When I entered and then finished my training in San Francisco as a Jungian analyst, it was mainly men and mainly MDs, so mainly people who were accepted in the collective as legitimate and qualified to practice. This was different from almost every other Jungian society except London. Here in Zurich, as you know, you could become a Jungian analyst without having a clinical background in psychology or psychotherapy. Jung liked that, and I like that. Some of those non-clinically trained people have been some of the best analysts around.

Murray: I agree. I think that's a value because you get diverse input into the field from many different directions. I remember when I came back from Zurich and we met at Carmel in 1974 for the first time saying that it seemed to me that training in the States was like "frosting on the cake."

Tom: Yes. I always remembered that. The word you used was "patina."

Murray: Yes, that's it. I felt it was merely a patina, because the people who at that time were being trained as Jungian analysts had already undergone such extensive clinical training and then it seemed to me they got a smattering of Jungian ideas that they might or might not use in their practices. Has that changed?

Tom: Oh, but that wasn't true!

Murray: Wasn't true?

Tom: That wasn't true. Our seminars were very Jungian.

Murray: Classical Jungian, not developmental? Did you tend more to the symbolic approach of Jung's Zurich or to childhood transference and the object relations approach of Fordham's London?

Tom: It was classical, not developmental. We had, for instance, eight sessions on Jung's "Psychology of the Transference" with Joe Henderson. We had Elizabeth Osterman lecturing on Esther Harding's *Women's Mysteries* and "The Symbolism of the Villa of Mysteries in Pompeii." We had John Perry giving eight seminars on the theory of complexes. All of it was very classical.

Murray: And you read Jung?

Tom: We read lots of Jung.

Murray: Somehow, I got a different impression.

Tom: I think it must have been who you talked to. I mean, I read most of Jung's works in my training. I read almost everything.

Murray: What about practice? You were in analysis with C.A. Meier, Jung's right hand man in Zurich. You could say he would have been the most classical of the classical analysts with his emphasis on dream interpretation and symbols. How was that different from what you experienced in your analysis with Joe Henderson? Was Jungian practice in California different at that time?

Tom: Let me tell you just a little bit about Joe Henderson. He was born in 1903, and this was before newborn babies routinely received silver nitrate in their eyes to prevent infection. He had an infection in one eye and lost his sight in that eye, but luckily the other eye's vision was saved. But what this meant was that he never had depth perception. He grew up on a ranch in Nevada, and he couldn't lasso cattle or play sports because he had no depth perception. So, he turned his perception inward. And he was a very introverted fellow, as you know. The person who got him into Jungian studies and inspired him to go to see Jung in Zurich was Peter Baynes, who was spending his sabbatical year in 1926-27 in California. Baynes gave him a copy of Jung's *The Seven Sermons to the Dead*! He read that and said: "I've got to go to Zurich, I've got to see this man." Baynes encouraged him to do it.

THOMAS B. KIRSCH IN CONVERSATION WITH MURRAY STEIN IN THE HOME OF C.G. JUNG

Murray: We are now at this moment in the very house where *The Seven Sermons to the Dead* were given! I imagine it might have been here in Jung's library where it was written down.

Tom: Yes, right here. And that little book is what got Joe Henderson over here to Zurich where he could study with Jung.

Murray: So, was your analysis with Joe Henderson similar to the one you had with C.A. Meier?

Tom: Very similar. Actually, if I may confess my transference to Henderson, he was better at dream interpretation than Meier. And his approach was very classical.

Murray: Do dreams still play an important role of your life?

Tom: It's interesting. No, they do not. Or rather, they've become less important, but on this trip I have had two or three really powerful dreams. I think these different medications for the cancer and the diabetes knocks out some of my dream life.

Murray: But dreams have been important to you in the past?

Tom: Absolutely.

Murray: Throughout your entire life?

Tom: Yes, for my whole life. I threw away a lot of my dream books because I didn't want anyone to see them. When Joe Henderson died, he left behind a lot of his dream books. I have them, but I've never opened them. I don't want to know more about his personal life than I learned from my personal interactions with him. I figure somebody else from a later generation who didn't know Joe can look at them and can investigate whatever is in there.

Murray: Can you mention one or two important dreams you've had, maybe dreams about Jung… but really significant, dreams that shaped your life in some way?
Tom: I had a dream when I was seeing Joe Henderson that I was going into a men's restroom, and there was a row of urinals. I found myself standing next to Jung. He looked like a young man and had, as he did in his younger years, a butch haircut. He was kind of an alter ego figure for me since I too was young at that time. He was urinating, and I was urinating. Joe Henderson and I talked about it as somehow a kind of power drive, as ambition … and this really affected me. In a sense, I was overly ambitious, probably pushed by my mother. And something happened to me in the course of my analysis with Henderson that was the very opposite. I identified more with Joe. Part of why I mentioned him last night and dedicated the lecture to him is because he never pushed himself forward.
Murray: Absolutely. As I knew him, he was a person who always held himself back.
Tom: He was very modest about what he did, in a sense. I've done a lot in the field, and Joe did a tremendous amount. There are times I could just get glossed over. This bothers me, but less now. I don't need it anymore.
Murray: The dream puts you beside Jung. Do you think Jung was ambitious?
Tom: Before he worked out the *Red Book*, before his confrontation with the unconscious, I think he was quite ambitious.
Murray: But after that not so much?
Tom: I don't think so, not afterwards. I think that experience changed him. But I think he was upset that

THOMAS B. KIRSCH IN CONVERSATION WITH MURRAY STEIN IN THE HOME OF C.G. JUNG

people didn't read him more and when they did read him, he felt misunderstood by them and thought they didn't really get what he meant by the unconscious and so forth.

Murray: Yes, I think that's important. Jung is not easy to read and he is sometimes hard to understand. I think that's one of the reasons why he isn't cited by a lot by people who would have an affinity with his thought but haven't really devoted themselves to his writings. You can't just pick him up and get it in a survey course. It takes a lifetime of study, really.

Tom: I agree.

Murray: You mentioned *The Red Book* just now. That was created right here in this room where we are sitting between 1913 and 1930. But it was published only in 2009, so many years later. It made a big splash in the public, with lots of conferences about it and now books and essays appearing about it, too. What do you think about the publication of *The Red Book*? Was it a good thing to do at this late date?

Tom: Before it was published, I wished it would not be published.

Murray: You didn't want to see it published?

Tom: That's right. I didn't want to see it. I thought, you know, this is Jung's personal diary. Even though it has a lot of very abstract and symbolic unconscious material in it, I thought, leave it alone, leave the poor guy alone, you know, let him have his personal diary. He didn't want it published. If he had wanted that published, he would have published it himself or given instructions to publish it after his death. But he didn't.

Murray: But he didn't destroy it either, and he did not say never to publish it.

Tom: He did not destroy it, but he was very ambivalent about it.

Murray: Have you read it?

Tom: Oh yes! All of it. I have read all of it more than once. I was on a radio program about it in San Francisco, very popular. I have spoken about it six or seven times.

Murray: I recall now that you were on the program in Washington at the Library of Congress when *The Red Book* was presented there. So, do you feel differently now that it has been published? Do you think it's a good thing that it's out there in public for everyone to read?

Tom: At first, I was afraid also of a possible negative effect it might have, because some of the symbolism is really hard to understand and hard to take.

Murray: Yes, I agree.

Tom: And hard to swallow, so I was really concerned about that. I thought it would hurt Jung's image, his reputation. And in fact, I have heard some negative things.

Murray: Some people, like Sonu Shamdasani, the book's editor, for instance, have made the claim that it's going to revolutionize the way we understand Jung. Do you think that's true?

Tom: No, not at all.

Murray: I agree with you. It adds some biographical connections, but it doesn't change anything essential in Jung's theory.

Tom: It adds, it amplifies, but it hasn't changed any basic understanding of Jung's ideas. Sonu is not an analyst, he is a historian, and for historians it's important to get documents out. So, it's another document to add to the corpus, but it is not anything revolutionary.

Murray: But do you think it gives people a stronger appreciation for the importance of active imagination in Jungian work? It is really an exercise of active imagination. There are a few dreams mentioned, but basically, it's all active imagination and commentary.

Tom: Murray, I have to tell you I am surprised you actually asked me if I read *The Red Book*…

Murray: Lots of people haven't, you know! They look at the pictures and don't read the text. But of course, I know that you read it thoroughly!

Tom: Actually, you and I had some discussions about it. You have made some really interesting comments about *The Red Book*, and I actually incorporated some of them into my talks. But I didn't enjoy reading it.

Murray: I didn't either at first.

Tom: Really?

Murray: No, I didn't. Parts of it I found hard to take and I had to close it.

Tom: I had to close it too.

Murray: It's a very strong stuff and unlike Jung's other writing.

Tom: It was just too much for me. I had to read two or three pages at a time. I read a lot of it at our country place up at Sea Ranch where it was really quiet and I could concentrate.

Murray: Talk about it a little bit. For instance, can you say something about active imagination and how *The Red Book* brings this method more into the foreground of Jungian analysis?

Tom: That's an interesting point. When I started analysis in the late '50s, all my analysts had drawing paper and color pencils next to where the analysand sat. And so actually when I started my practice, I did the same thing. The idea was that you had to draw, draw your dream images as a kind of active imagination within the hour. Especially when you had a particularly strong dream, you would draw it.

Murray: That's interesting. So, you did that with Meier and Henderson?

Tom: Oh, yes. I wasn't that big on active imagination, but I did some; I also did some writing, some inner dialogue. That was a big thing in those days.

Murray: Do you think it more or less got lost later?

Tom: Yes, it got lost. It got lost; it got lost, absolutely. And so, obviously, *The Red Book* has brought that back into the picture.

Murray: You see there what Jung did by way of inner dialogue and image making.

Tom: But I don't think that many Jungians have gone back to doing active imagination on a very regular basis. There was something about it ... if I may say... that it was kind of following Jung too closely ... you know, kind of imitating Jung rather than doing one's own thing.

Murray: Well, on that point, how have Jungian training and practices changed since you began in the '50s? Would you comment on that? I mean, you have seen it all over the world, too, not only in the United States, but in all your travels internationally.

Tom: I have seen how the training in San Francisco has changed, and there's a new interesting development.

THOMAS B. KIRSCH IN CONVERSATION WITH MURRAY STEIN IN THE HOME OF C.G. JUNG

One of our training groups is coming over to Zurich for a visit with some analysts here.

Murray: They want "a taste of Zurich."

Tom: They want to know what it was like earlier and what it is like now to be in Zurich, because the Zurich training is so much more image oriented than it is in San Francisco where it's much more focused on dynamic psychotherapy and transference. I think it behooves us somehow in San Francisco to develop what I would call an inter-relational subjective analytic approach with a big emphasis on dreams and the unconscious, a dialogue with the foundation in the collective unconscious. But that hasn't been solidified, so far. We do much more in San Francisco now with the developmental school, Fordham, attachment theory, and things like that. We had none of that when I was a candidate; it was all classical Jung. Things changed when Heinz Kohut came to the fore. We added Kohut to the syllabus, and then there were two or three people who went to see Fordham in London and they brought his approach back with them. Fordham then came and spent a month with us in 1981 or '82. I think that he impressed a number of analysts, and that changed a lot of things. But in London at the Society of Analytical Psychology (SAP), for instance, if you look at the reading list, there's almost no Jung. They are not required to read Jung. Lots for Fordham, lots of the developmental material, but almost nothing by Jung appears on the reading list.

Murray: Last night in your lecture you said that Freud has become a historical figure, meaning a figure of the past that nobody studies all that seriously anymore. But some still do, only outside the training institutes, that

is, philosophers and historians rather than clinicians. Do you think that's happening to Jung nowadays as well?
Tom: No. I think, in a way, and now I'm exaggerating a little, the 20th century was Freudian and the 21st could be Jungian. All this extremism, all this religiosity, it's all a version of the collective unconscious in a way. I know that's a simplistic thing to say, but we need Jung to address to these issues. I don't know if you agree with that or not.
Murray: I do find Jung helpful for speaking about collective issues and cultural matters. I know I think it can be oversimplified though, you know, and so not very helpful, but I think for some things and used well it can be very helpful. I think Jung has been held up as the psychologist of the 21st century because is more amenable to postmodernism than he was to modernism, that is, to the kind of loosening of collective attitudes and more emphasis on diffuse and multiple identities and complexities in the psyche—not so ego oriented, not so straight. There is room for multiplicity to come out and be expressed in the individual and the collective. This is what Jung offers us for reflection. For instance, there is the whole issue of gender identity that is so up in the air these days with people opting for gender complexity or gender change that totally offends the traditionalists and conservatives. Jung's theory of anima and animus teaches us that we are complex when it comes to gender identity, that is not a simple and stable thing. This is a feature of postmodernism. I do hope Jung doesn't become only a historical figure. He has so much to offer.
Tom: I hope too.

THOMAS B. KIRSCH IN CONVERSATION WITH MURRAY STEIN IN THE HOME OF C.G. JUNG

Murray: This building that we are sitting in, Jung's own house, was designed and built by him and Emma in 1909, and it will become a museum in a couple of years. This will become a part of history in an official way, and this library will be an archive of his intellectual interests.
Tom: Really, that soon?
Murray: Yes, that's the plan. It will take place in the latter part of 2017. People will be invited to come here and look around and spend some time, under carefully controlled conditions. It will be something like the Freud Museum in London, along those lines. But when you start creating museums, you know, maybe you're saying Jung is now historical, maybe no longer so relevant to the times people are living in. He enters the museum world of old artifacts to admire, and maybe this could take away his value as a still living force somewhat. But do you think the spirit of Jung still lives in our training institutes and analyst societies?
Tom: Somewhat.
Murray: Yes, and sometimes it become only a patina.
Tom: Yes.
Murray: Is there a danger that we will lose the spirit of Jung?
Tom: I do think there is a danger that we will lose it. In the United States today there's such an emphasis on quick fixes. The idea of long-term therapy and analysis is a little low right now. I mean, if I had to open a practice today, I would not see myself filling up so quickly because people just aren't looking for analysis, they want quick fixes, they want drugs, they want cognitive behavioral therapy and its offer of fast and painless results.

Murray: Five sessions, presto! You're healed! Back to work!

Tom: Yes. I think Jungians are suffering because of that. I feel that the time that I've been a practicing analyst, which is almost 50 years, was kind of a heyday for long-term therapy.

Murray: That's right, it was very popular, everybody had to have an analyst and see them regularly. But did it make a difference? Jim Hillman wrote a book some years ago, *We've Had a Hundred Years of Psychotherapy - And Things Are Getting Worse.* Did it make a difference in the big scheme of things that people had extensive analysis? I certainly think it did make a difference on the collective level. It raised consciousness in the culture. When you think of all the artists, authors, intellectuals and also people in all other walks of life who had this experience, it adds up to a profound cultural influence.

Tom: I like to think that my analysis made a big difference to my life.

Murray: On a personal level.

Tom: Yes, on a personal level.

Murray: And we don't know what our culture would be like if we hadn't had all that analysis.

Tom: That's right.

Murray: It could have gone to hell much sooner than it seems to be going now?

Tom: Right, so I say it's personal for me, it made a change in my life, but it also permitted me to get out in the world and impart the experience that I had in my own analysis to others. You know, just by being, hopefully being myself, and I think that's happened with a lot of people who have had an analysis.

THOMAS B. KIRSCH IN CONVERSATION WITH MURRAY STEIN IN THE HOME OF C.G. JUNG

Murray: Yes, I think in your travels you have affected a lot of people. You started the Jungian interest in Taiwan a few years ago, for instance, and a lot of people have been affected.

Tom: But the Jungian position is a minority position and I can't see it becoming mainstream. Doing seminars and workshops and so forth, you realize how hard it is to get people to come out for them. You just don't reach a lot of people, you don't get big audiences usually. There was a time in the 60s and 70s when Jung was very "in," fashionable. When I first became an analyst in the 60s, we had a dream seminar at the University of California extension with 600 or 700 people attending. And regularly we would have 300 or 400 coming to events in those days.

Murray: Large numbers.

Tom: It was amazing! And now if we have seminars at the institute and 50 people attend, we're tickled pink.

Murray: A lot of books have been written by Jungian analysts, and one hopes they make something of a difference on a broad cultural level. You've written two major books. History is your special interest, isn't it? *The Jungians* was written after your presidency, and that's done very well in sales, lots of people buy it, refer to it, and use it. You really covered the spectrum in that work. How was it writing that book for you?

Tom: It is 20 years since I started really writing it. It was a way for me to express my views of the IAAP in part, but also it allowed me to talk about my earlier experience here in Zurich, in New York, Los Angeles, and San Francisco. Those were the groups that I knew the best.

Murray: You also traveled quite a lot and you did a lot of research for that book.

Tom: Yes, I went to almost every society that was existent at that time.

Murray: When was it published?

Tom: It was published in 2000. It's interesting because when I was ready to turn it in, Ursula Egli, who was my IAAP secretary, said to me: "Tom, you have to go through the whole book once again, you have to re-do the whole thing. You have to go over the whole thing again." I was really flattened by that. And so, for one entire month we spent several hours every day going over the text. And what she picked up was that I used the same word in it repetitively, very unconsciously.

Murray: Sure, you don't think about these things when you're writing. Somebody else reads it and they see it.

Tom: So, she read it and we made a lot of changes.

Murray: Now it's been 16 years since it was published. Has the picture changed much?

Tom: Where the picture has changed is in Central and South America and in Asia—China, Japan, Taiwan, Korea. I would add Israel, where there are three groups now. The publisher asked me if I would want to make a second revised edition, and if I had the energy I would. But I don't, and I can't do it.

Murray: Yes, that would be a big job.

Tom: It's for someone else to update what's going on.

Murray: Regarding more recent developments, you well know that one is often asked what's happening in the Jungian world. I think it's flourishing in some ways. It's a little stagnant in the developed areas maybe, but there

THOMAS B. KIRSCH IN CONVERSATION WITH MURRAY STEIN IN THE HOME OF C.G. JUNG

are other parts that are really growing and there is a lot of interest.

Tom: It is, it is. And again, I am going to refer back to San Francisco. In San Francisco, when I became a candidate, I was told that it would hurt me from getting any kind of academic position or any of the position in psychiatry.

Murray: To become a Jungian analyst?

Tom: Yes, that I was making a mistake in my career. Today many people come into the San Francisco Institute, it is no longer marginal, and it's respected. And I mean not only by Jungians, but by the collective in the Bay Area. So, if you say you are a candidate in San Francisco Jung Institute, it actually raises you up in people's estimation, and that's a huge change in attitude. And as a matter of fact, the candidates from both the psychoanalytic institutes, all the psychoanalytic institutes, and the Jungians get together now for various occasions.

Murray: Do you think that there will be a convergence of schools? It can't be a reunion or something like that, because Jungians and psychoanalysts are so basically different in their assumptions.

Tom: They are not going to merge.

Murray: I agree. We have people like Don Kalsched, who is very conversant with a lot of psychoanalytic theories, and he weaves them together to an extent, but at the end of the day he is a Jungian. He speaks about soul and self in a very Jungian way.

Tom: Oh, absolutely.

Murray: And I think the other schools can't go there. They could go with us a few miles, but then…

Tom: And then they stop.

Murray: They stop, yes. I think it's the sense of the spiritual, you know, the archetypal elements of the psyche; when we get into that kind of language and talk they just tune out and leave.

Tom: They don't like it.

Murray: And now as you are approaching your final years—nobody knows how many more they have—but you know, you are 80 now, let's hope you have many more still to come, but who knows? How do you relate to the spiritual at this stage of your life? Is it any different? Do you think about death, life after death, do you believe in God? I could ask you that famous question. Jung sitting right here, when he was asked that question: "Do you believe in God?" And he gave his famous answer, "I do not believe, I know." What is your take on that sort of question now?

Tom: That's a difficult question. A profound question. When I got on this experimental drug study for the kidney cancer, and I saw that it was working, I said to myself, there is some spirit behind all this. I was the last person to be accepted for this study, they were ready to close it to any new patients. And then it worked! I don't know how long it will continue to work but, you know, the fact that it's worked has made me a strong ... what can I say? ...a believer of the spirit? In a way I felt that before, but this really strengthens it. Before I started that drug and before I got accepted into this program, when I first got the diagnosis of kidney cancer, my reaction was, okay, I have done a lot, I feel I have had a satisfactory life. I just said, that's it, you know.

Murray: And you were ready to accept it.

THOMAS B. KIRSCH IN CONVERSATION WITH MURRAY STEIN IN THE HOME OF C.G. JUNG

Tom: I was ready to accept it. You know, it's disappeared a little, it is gone, receded into the background now that I feel better again. I read a book by Tom Brokaw about his multiple myeloma, and the things that he said about what he felt about his disease in that book mirrored so much what happened to me. There is an uncertainty that one has...

Murray: You cannot count on the next day.

Tom: You cannot count on it, right. And, you know, people say we are all live with uncertainty. But when you've got a disease going on inside you that you know can kill you at any time, you...

Murray: You feel helpless.

Tom: Yes. And that's not quite as close to me now. Actually, it's closer to me right now. It wasn't before coming here, but I knew that, in a way, coming here, as you say, this may be very well be my last trip here, you know, and it puts me into that kind of perspective.

Murray: Yes. Do you have any thoughts about life after death?

Tom: No, I don't think about that at all.

Murray: Not at all. So, you don't expect to see your mother and father?

Tom: No, I don't think about that. I mean, I do think about my mother and my father, and I had long relationships with both of them.

Murray: Do you feel close to them still?

Tom: Do I feel close to them? Thank God I feel more distant from them! I mean, I feel a tremendous amount of love for them, but writing a memoir of my life brought up material about my parents that I'd never expected. I wish my analysts were still alive, because I'd never been conscious of the feelings I had about them. My mother was a patient of my father's. She married him out of a transference, and they never worked it out. They really never worked out their relationship in a satisfactory fashion. And I think it was sad for both of them.

Murray: So, you felt some sadness for them?

Tom: Oh, yes! And I'm going through all the old pictures now, and I see so many photos of my mother where she looks so sad and depressed. It's hard to look at them

Murray: It's the problem with the transference enactment, isn't it? You don't get what you think you see there.

Tom: Exactly, and to a much greater extent than in the usual situation which is also filled with a lot of projection, but it's not the same as in the transference. My parents almost got divorced when I was 15, but they finally got together again. At that time, I was relieved, but I thought many times afterwards what it would have been like for them to have really made that separation.

Murray: The theme of separation has been very important in your life.

Tom: Oh, yes, oh very... I know I have a deep fear of abandonment. I don't know why, since my mother especially was very close. But I know one time that I hurt her very much. I was asked when I was 10 or 11 years old to write a biography of my parents. And I very innocently wrote that my mother is a psychologist who is also secondarily a mother. That really got her! You know, in retrospect I can see why ... she was very upset when she saw that paper.

Murray: But maybe she was so dedicated to her patients that you felt in second place sometimes.

THOMAS B. KIRSCH IN CONVERSATION WITH MURRAY STEIN IN THE HOME OF C.G. JUNG

Tom: In some ways. But she brought me into her patient's sessions. She would talk about me with her patients. It was very embarrassing because when I was younger, I would go to these different places and give a talk and people would come up after the lecture and say, "You know, I heard about you from your mother because I was a patient of hers." I didn't enjoy that.

Murray: Changing topics now, I'd like to ask you about something you spoke of earlier. You said that you were pulling back somewhat from commitments like giving lectures and seminars. When Jo Wheelwright, the other extrovert among us, took his leave and retired, he really disappeared, didn't he? He went out to his ranch and cut all the contacts. It was a pretty radical separation.

Tom: Oh, yes, he did.

Murray: Are you planning anything like that?

Tom: No! I hope to continue living in Palo Alto and we have a house on the coast and I continue to participate in activities at the Institute in San Francisco. But I can feel less libido, less energy for many things. I don't care about as many things, or as many people, or about what's going on in the Jungian world. It doesn't have quite the same energy as it did earlier.

Murray: Has something replaced all that?

Tom: Well, I want to take it easy, I want to read, I am a sports fan, I love sports. I played sports growing up, much to my parents' chagrin, I mean the extent to which I did it. They were worried about me.

Murray: And what now? Do you watch baseball? I know you are a baseball fan.

Tom: I watch baseball. I love to go to baseball games, and I am watching some professional basketball. I watch some tennis.
Murray: And music, I know you have loved music all your life.
Tom: I go to a lot of concerts.
Murray: You like music live.
Tom: I like it live. I like it much better live than listening to home stereo.
Murray: Well, now let me ask you about Jung. Has Jung, the man, changed for you in all these years?
Tom: Oh, God yes, he has changed a lot for me. Back then, you know, I was quite identified with him, and I feel very fortunate that I met Joe Henderson. In retrospect, I look at all the people who were that part of that first generation of Jungians who came to Jung between the end of the First World War and the beginning of the Second World War; people like Michael Fordham, Adler, my parents, Henderson, Wheelwright, Neumann, and a lot of others—and I think that Joe Henderson was the least caught up in an identification with Jung himself. For instance, when Jung wrote him a letter and he answered it, he threw away Jung's letter. "Okay, I have answered it," was his thought. (On the other hand, when you and I first met Andreas and Vreni Jung, and Vreni told us that there is this correspondence between Jung and Joe Henderson, I got it for Joe. Joe at that time was 100, 102 actually, and they got it to him very quickly. He was very excited about it. That was probably the last intellectual thing that he was excited about in his long life.) So, I felt that having Joe Henderson as my analyst helped me to become dis-identified.

THOMAS B. KIRSCH IN CONVERSATION WITH MURRAY STEIN IN THE HOME OF C.G. JUNG

Murray: Yes, I see. That helped you get some distance from Jung.

Tom: And then I became good friends with Andrew Samuels, and I heard all about the shadow of Jung! I mean it was way exaggerated, in my opinion, but I heard it. And it affected me too, because there was something in it. I guess over time the most prominent thing that I feel about Jung was that Jung became a symbol for me, a symbol of individuality. I didn't have to read all of alchemy, I didn't have to be a scholar of alchemy...

Murray: You did not have to imitate Jung.

Tom: I did not have to imitate Jung, that was the thing. And as great a person as he was, I had to find my own way. And I have.

Murray: What do you think about him now?

Tom: I think he had tremendous insights about the human psyche and about the world we live in, and I wish people would read him more and understand him more. I really do.

Murray: So, you feel he has something to offer to the world in his writings...

Tom: Oh, yes, absolutely. But I don't have the push to be the one to impart that word to the public.

Murray: What word would you want to impart?

Tom: That's a good question. I think that Jung is a symbol of individuality, of individuation. That's what I want to impart. And that was very hard-earned and hard for me to accept. You know, I was not a Jungian scholar like you are, I'm not that, I mean I do a lot of reading, I am smart, but it's just not where I want to put my energy.

Murray: But what would you like to leave as your testament to the younger generations coming along?
Tom: I wrote *The Jungians* because I felt that, in my own way, I had an overall picture of the Jungian world that very few other people have. From my early life on I have been in the middle of it, and I wanted to impart that as impartially and as objectively as I could without getting into a lot of polemics. That was important for me to do. And the memoir, *A Jungian Life*, was also a way of talking about how it was to be a Jungian and how that changed over my lifetime.
Murray: So, you have left your testament in these two books.
Tom: Yes, I think I have left my testament in these two books.
Murray: Do you ever regret having becoming a Jungian analyst?
Tom: I don't think I've ever regretted it, but I have questioned why I did it. You know, I mean, was it really my own, or it was really at the bottom because of a push from my mother? Certainly, it was not my father's influence that made me an analyst. For me it was an acquired taste. I mean I really had to work at it for myself. My father was a rather narcissistic man and he was not particularly related to being a father, although he was very generous in many ways. For instance, he introduced me to Jung, and he allowed me these many connections to his friends and colleagues.
Murray: But it was all about Jung, somehow, wasn't it? Your father's life was all about Jung.
Tom: His life was all about Jung.
Murray: Not about you primarily.

THOMAS B. KIRSCH IN CONVERSATION WITH MURRAY STEIN IN THE HOME OF C.G. JUNG

Tom: Yes, much more about Jung than about me.
Murray: If you had done something other than going into the Jungian field, what would you have chosen?
Tom: I loved of all things about medicine, like biochemistry and endocrinology. I found endocrinology a fascinating subject and that certainly would've been an option.
Murray: Would you have been a researcher?
Tom: I think not, because of my typology. I would have enjoyed clinical practice and having patients. I've enjoyed having a practice, being an analyst for 48 years. I don't talk about that much, but I had a full practice for 45 years.
Murray: And very interesting patients.
Tom: Some very interesting patients, some not so interesting. I've had a big variety and I enjoyed it.
Murray: Is there something you would especially like to talk about in the time that's left?
Tom: What I would like to do is tell you one dream that I had this week. It's the one dream I had, and it was in the Tessin before coming here to Zurich. I woke up scared, I was panicked in the dream. The dream was that I was in a building that had a Macintosh stereo, not a Macintosh computer, but Macintosh stereo, which is a very high-end, very high-quality musical sound. That was very big earlier, and it is still around but with all the movie and multimedia stuff now it is not quite as prominent. But this was the prominent thing, and I was in India. Suddenly I was going to take an airplane, but instead of being in an airplane I was being pulled by a rope very quickly along a path and finally got into the airplane. It was a commercial airplane, and it was very

scary. Then my wife leaves me. This is the theme I have had all my life, this theme of abandonment. And when I realize that she leaves me, I panic. I'm in India, and I'm all alone. Then I awaken. It woke me up in the middle of the night. I remember in the early part of my analysis with Joe I would have dreams of flying high. I haven't had one for a long time. My association was that here I was giving this Jung Memorial Lecture, and for me that was a big deal. There were a lot of people there, and I felt that it was well received. I was concerned about my ambition again, climbing and trying to get too high.

Murray: Being pulled to fly.

Tom: Being pulled. And my Indian anima, which would be my introverted, Eastern meditative side, would abandon me. I'd lose it. I would get too extroverted and be pulled along ... too ambitious again. I spent quite a bit of time thinking about it, and I thought, well, probably this is related to coming to Zurich and giving this lecture, you know, which is significant, and then there is going to be this interview today. It's going to put me in the spotlight again. I've withdrawn a lot from being in the spotlight.

Murray: Now you have to go in search of your soul again.

Tom: Yes. So that's how I looked at the dream.

Murray: Well, it seems that you're still in touch with your dreams, you use them, you think about them, you reflect on your life through them and with them.

Tom: I do.

Murray: And that's the Jungian way, isn't it? With your illness now, has the Jungian approach been of help in dealing with it?

THOMAS B. KIRSCH IN CONVERSATION WITH MURRAY STEIN IN THE HOME OF C.G. JUNG

Tom: I cannot specifically say how, but one of the things about Joe Henderson who lived to be 104 left with me as a legacy is to live life as it comes. We talked about death, and that he didn't consciously think about life after death or about approaching death. He just lived his life from day to day. And I have taken that attitude on for myself.
Murray: Yes, I think you have.
Tom: Day to day ... not thinking about it.
Murray: I can see Joe in you. When Joe was about your age, I asked him: "Joe, do you think a lot about death, do you worry about it?" He said: "No, you know, in my 60s and 70s, I thought quite a lot about it, but I don't anymore."
Tom: Yes, it's that attitude that he imparted.
Murray: I think you received it, you picked it up.
Tom: I have taken it in as much as I can. You know that.

From L to R: Franck Guillemain, Andreas Jung, Murray Stein, Thomas Singer, Luis Moris.

Murray: One day at a time, every day.
Tom: Yes.
Murray: Tom, this has been very nice conversation in Jung's study.
Tom: Oh yes, I would agree.
Murray: I feel very close to you, and I feel like you really shared yourself and have been available, and as always, open and humble and yourself.
Tom: Thank you. I'm glad you were the interviewer.
Murray: This has been a nice experience.
Tom: This has been a very satisfying experience. So, thank you.
Murray: Thank you.

Tom Kirsch:
A Man for All Seasons
by Thomas Singer

"The undiscovered vein within us is a living part of the psyche; classical Chinese philosophy names this interior way 'Tao,' and likens it to a flow of water that moves irresistibly towards its goal. To rest in Tao means fulfillment, wholeness, one's destination reached, one's mission done; the beginning, end, and perfect realization of the meaning of existence innate in all things. Personality is Tao." C.G. Jung. CW.17.§23.

I used to enjoy—more than enjoy really—I used to love being with Tom Kirsch, which often included speaking on the phone a couple of times a week for many years. The topics of our conversations ranged from family matters to international, national, and local Jungian affairs, from sports news to vexing clinical problems, from the latest spy novel we had read to any number of ARAS projects that we cared about (The Archive for Research in Archetypal Symbolism). We talked about the obscure or forgotten historical personages of our Jungian tradition, the complexities and trials of leadership, and the occasional pain of feeling that we had not been recognized for the value of our work. We both had an abundance of attention from our mothers and that "positive mother complex" sometimes made it hard for us not to feel rejected if the world didn't treat us the same way. We talked about matters of life and death, soul and spirit, and the weak relief pitching staffs of the St. Louis Cardinals and the San Francisco Giants baseball teams. It is still hard for me to believe that Tom is not here and that we are not talking frequently about the greatest challenges of our times and the smallest annoyances of everyday life.

Tom had many good friends; he was very good at friendship. And yet, Tom made me feel as if I were a special friend and I think many people felt that way. Tom always greeted me with a hearty, booming "TOM SINGER." Not even my mother greeted me with such warm affection—as if each time we came together it was an unexpected surprise and delight for Tom to see me. His greeting made me feel so welcomed and embraced in his presence.

In his poignant remarks at Tom's memorial service, Andrew Samuels focused on Tom's courage, intelligence, and beauty as among the defining characteristics of his unique being. Rarely spoken about—especially in and among men—is the quality of physical beauty in men. Tom was beautiful—inside and outside. He was quietly charismatic. He was tall and good looking. His face was both lovely and kindly. His body was always fit as a result of his dedicated swimming routine and he was comfortable in his body. Tom had a naturally dignified bearing which made him easy to spot in a room, and there was a calming comfort about being in his presence.

Tom brought decency, integrity, grounded worldliness, great intelligence, and depth of feeling to the clinical practice of Jungian analysis, to the teaching of Jungian theory and practice, to the study of Jungian history, and to the international development and diplomacy of the Jungian tradition. He will be remembered for all of these considerable accomplishments.

Above all, Tom was a very warm-hearted man, and not just to me but to many, many people. He always greeted my wife, Jane, with genuine fondness which made her feel at home even when the Jungian world was not her natural habitat. The phrase that keeps coming to me as I try to conjure up in words what he meant to me is: "Tom was a man for all seasons." I found these rather weak definitions[9] of "a man for all seasons":

1. A man who is ready to cope with any contingency and whose behavior is always appropriate to every occasion

2. A man who is successful and talented in many areas

As is often the case, the definition somehow misses the essential meaning of the phrase and certainly doesn't do justice to what "a man of all seasons" means to me when I use it to describe Tom Kirsch's fully lived life and my friendship with him. "All seasons" certainly suggests not only every occasion, but every stage of life.

---

[9] https://idioms.thefreedictionary.com/a+man+for+all+seasons

I think it can also refer to all the different passions of a lively, curious soul.

Tom had so many interests that he pursued vigorously and well. With his parents having fled Nazi Germany to London, where he was born, and then emigrating to Los Angeles in the late 1940s four, Tom was steeped in the history and culture of Europe. In some ways, Europe remained a center of gravity for him all his life. But not the only one. With his growing interest in Taiwan and China in later life and his previous sixteen years of travel as a member of the Executive Committee and then president of the IAAP, Tom traveled the globe: Latin America, Australia, Western Europe, South Africa, Israel, Russia, and many other places. Tom truly became a "wandering Jew" in his own, unique way. At the same time, as a youth, he identified strongly with being an American and, somewhat against his parents' wishes for him, he became fascinated with sports. Tom was an avid tennis player until back surgery ended that career. He was a swimmer until almost the very end of his life. And, he became a devoted baseball fan with an unfailing loyalty to the San Francisco Giants. In the tradition of Chaim Potok's *The Chosen*, becoming a baseball fan was the quickest and perhaps easiest way to assimilate into American culture, and Tom passed that test of becoming a first generation, immigrant American—as he did almost every other test in his life—with flying colors.

There was a lovely story that Tom told me on more than one occasion about a meeting with Bob Feller whose nickname was "The Heater from Van Meter" as Feller was born in Van Meter, Iowa, an archetypal place of Midwestern American origins. Feller, a Baseball Hall of Famer, was one of the greatest pitchers in the history of the game. One year, Tom took his grandson, Jacob, to the Giants' spring training in Arizona. Feller was there, too—seated at a table signing autographs. For Tom to meet Bob Feller was almost as big a deal for Tom as to have met with C.G. Jung as a young man. Tom had already been welcomed into the Jungian "family" by Jung who sent James and Hilde Kirsch a note of congratulations on Tom's birth. So, Tom was destined to be a Jungian from the very beginning and, as he was fond of saying, he "went into the family business." But, for Tom to become a lifelong baseball fan on his own initiative was not necessarily in the family plans for him. The fact is that Tom may have remembered more of his few-minute meeting with Feller than he did his hour-long private meeting as a young man with Jung. In any case, Tom, with his grandson at his side, found himself face-to-face with a childhood hero of Titanic proportions. Jacob related the story of that meeting at Tom's memorial service in San Francisco in 2017. What Jacob remembers most vividly is that Tom made such an easy, natural connection with Feller that they lingered in conversation for several minutes. Jacob was deeply impressed by Tom's being totally at ease with such a famous man. But, the fact is that Tom could be at ease with almost anybody—famous or not. And he could put at ease almost anybody he was engaged with.

Perhaps more rooted in his European origins, Tom developed a passion for and knowledge of classical music. It was one of the few areas that I could not follow

Tom. Although my last name is Singer, I have no musical ability whatsoever and even less feel for classical music. So, I could only marvel at and envy Tom's love of music. He had an incredible memory for concerts (and just about everything else) that he attended throughout his life. He could name the performer, the piece they played, the date and place of the performance. Music was as etched in his being as was being a Jungian. I think Tom's love of music reminded me of my own limitations in comparison to the breadth and depth of Tom's range. Tom had a huge range—of colleagues and friends, of travels, of interests, of accomplishments, of human experience. And yet, he always had an essential modesty about him that suited him well.

Perhaps one limitation that Tom had was evident in his surprising sense of inferiority about his intellectual achievements and the way in which that distorted his otherwise impeccable objectivity about himself and other people. I only came to know about that over time because it was not obvious or on the surface. And one of the ways I came to recognize it was in Tom's reactions to papers and books that I worked on. I learned not to expect much praise from Tom when I asked him to look at a paper or manuscript that I was in the midst of writing. Of course, I always wanted him to say that my work was original, insightful, and worthy of praise. But the fact is that Tom's booming greetings of me were far warmer than his responses to my writing. Tom was very allergic to inflation and, for a while, I thought he was trying to give me a lesson in creating something and not getting inflated about it. But, as I came to know Tom better, I realized that his way of knowing and being in the world was quite different from that of his highly intellectual father who had an introverted, intuitive thinking brilliance. Tom was more extroverted, and although there was nothing wrong with his thinking or intelligence, it didn't have the numinous charge that Jungians love in their "thought leaders"—to use an awful, contemporary phrase that somehow fits what our tradition tends to value most highly. Although Tom wrote several books and over 100 papers, he did not feel his work was regarded that highly and, in that sense, he lived a bit in the shadow of his father's intellectual achievements or, at least, what Tom perceived as his father's superior mind. For that reason, I think it was hard for Tom to praise too highly another's work— or at least mine. Of course, I could be quite wrong about this and Tom's lack of praise for my work was that he didn't think that highly of it and that it didn't deserve the praise I was coveting. But I do know that Tom was suspicious of the high-flying Jungian intellectuals, perhaps partly out of envy that he couldn't do it in that way and perhaps partly out of his knowing that such brilliance often ended in inflation and all the problems of human relatedness that grow out of an inflated narcissism.

Tom himself literally flew around the globe for many years and developed a wonderful appetite for adventure—for meeting new people in new places. What helped keep him grounded in his high-flying days was his relationship with Joe Henderson. Joe, a senior Jungian analyst who actually analyzed with Jung, was the most introverted man I have ever met. As a young man in my mid-20s, a baby Jungian really, my analyst arranged for me to stay with Dr. Henderson at his rented house near Bailey Island, Maine, for the celebration of Esther Harding's 80th birthday in 1968. I rode to and from the daily conferences with Dr. Henderson and we literally never said a word to one another on the 20- to 30-minute ride to and from the meetings. Later on, I too, ended up working with Joe for many years, and that made Tom and me analytic brothers, of a sort. Rather than create a rivalry between us, it joined us in the sense of having shared in being with one of the most remarkable people either one of us had ever known. We both loved baseball and tennis; we both attended Yale Medical School, although at different times; we both analyzed with Joe Henderson; and we both honored the Jungian tradition while recognizing its need to grow and evolve.

For years, Tom not only flew around the world but also had many dreams of flying. In his later years, he often found himself in his dreams hanging onto the tail of the plane as it was taking off. Although Tom continued to fly most of his life, Joe helped Tom ground himself. He also helped Tom separate from the incestuous identity he had with the Los Angeles Jungian tradition through his mother and father and find his own unique identity in Northern California. And, most of all, Joe helped Tom discover something of a still center in himself and in his relationship with Joe. Joe had a still center. I remember Tom describing his accompanying Joe very late in his life on a ten-hour flight from San Francisco to deliver a talk in London. In some amazement, Tom described how Joe buckled himself into the airplane seat and spent the next ten hours quietly looking straight ahead, without any agitation and without any need for the stimulation of a book, of a conversation, of a movie. He was perfectly comfortable sitting still for hours at a time. This quality of Joe's was enormously helpful to Tom in centering in his own inner reality and finding his own thoughts and feelings. Joe helped Tom center himself and not get too carried away by anything—except perhaps the Giants winning the World Series in 2010, 2012, and 2014.

When Tom eventually did stop flying around the world on IAAP business, he continued to travel to Taiwan to teach and to Europe for visits with old friends and to new beautiful places. With less travel and fewer international responsibilities, Tom turned his ever-keen curiosity to the history of the Jungian tradition. Born to two Jungian analysts and born into the almost family world of the 20th century Jungian tradition, Tom knew more about the history and development of the Jungian tradition in a firsthand way than probably anyone else in the world. And, so he applied his considerable intelligence and judgment to researching and writing about that history. His book, *The Jungians: A Comparative and Historical Perspective*, is a comprehensive social and intellectual history of the Jungian movement. His historical writing included the history of his own family and particularly some of the more painful aspects of his father's life as an analyst that involved more than one boundary-breaking affair with patients. Tom showed remarkable courage in dealing directly and publicly with the flaws of his father. This could not have been easy for him, and it took a big toll, as did dealing with the painful conflicts between the Jungian and

Freudian traditions, for which Tom became a featured spokesperson in his attempts to bridge the two traditions. He often had to defend Jung and the Jungian tradition against the unrelenting Freudian accusations of Jung's alleged anti-Semitism. In Versailles, where Tom spoke to an audience of mostly Freudian analysts, Tom was like a sheep in the lion's den as some of the Jewish Freudians attending the conference confronted Tom quite forcefully in their belief that Jung was directly responsible for the deaths of their own family members in the Holocaust. They believed that Jung was sympathetic to Naziism and supported Hitler. Tom never backed down from trying to discover and deliver as objective a perspective as possible on the Freudian critics of Jung. He was steadfast throughout his life in trying to present his point of view as a Jewish Jungian whose family had fled Germany and, at the same time, honored Jung and his tradition. Even in medical school at Yale which has had a strong Jewish Freudian tradition in its Department of Psychiatry, Tom was told by his well-intentioned advisors that he would be committing professional suicide and ruin his career before it started if he "came out" as a Jungian.

From a typological perspective, Tom's strength was not introverted, intuitive thinking, which has, perhaps, been the most prized in our tradition. Tom was extroverted, intuitive, and feeling—at least that is my sense of how we might think about him typologically. What served Tom incredibly well as an analyst, an international Jungian statesman, a family man, and a deep and loyal friend to many—Jungians and non-Jungians alike—was his incredibly finely tuned feeling, which was a trustworthy measure of the meaning and value of whatever the person or issue might be. Tom Kirsch lived a large and full life with travel, professional engagements, a love of music, sports, spy novels, and deep friendships around the world. In the midst of such expansive energies, he remained fundamentally modest, curious, open, and acutely discriminating in his many relationships to the world—inner and outer.

Tom was a mentor to me and much more. What I gleaned from the many confidences that he shared with me was a remarkable "in-tuneness" with what was most important and motivating to those around him. In today's language, we might say that he was a "relational" being. He had an almost uncanny ability to size up a person and a situation, which I came to trust in almost all circumstances. It certainly served him well in his leadership roles in our local San Francisco Jungian Institute, in his devoted work with ARAS, in his judgement in all sorts of difficult human situations as a clinician and also as a leader in our international community. He had a way of finding out what was going on, what was most important, where one needed to be cautious or, on the other side, to embrace a new person or situation. At the same time, he could maintain a personable persona while distancing himself and being objective about a situation that didn't "smell" right to him. Rarely did I see him give up on a person or a situation, but he could, with great struggle, decide that he needed to remove himself from a relationship that had gone sour or didn't deserve his emotional energy and time.

As a man for all seasons, Tom was prepared for almost every event, including his own death. I was profoundly impressed by the way Tom faced the autumn and winter of his life. He had both the burden and luxury of having a long time to prepare for his death as the kidney cancer that eventually took his life was well controlled for several years, although the eventual outcome was clear once Tom learned that the initial cancer had spread beyond his kidney. The progression of his disease was accompanied by a profoundly moving development in his psyche as he learned to live with the reality that death could come at any time. He faced that approaching certainty as he did everything else in his life—with careful preparation, clarity, grace, and the profound humanity of a deeply feeling man. In his final task of preparing for death, Tom was simply remarkable.

I had the great honor of visiting with Tom several times in the few months before his death. Driving from my home in Marin County down to Palo Alto had always seemed like an insurmountable distance to me before, even though Tom and Jean took the long drive from their home to San Francisco as part of their everyday life and commitment to our Jungian community. But as it became clear that Tom's days were numbered, I began to drive down to Palo Alto frequently and the drive got shorter and shorter in terms of my experience of time and distance. And every time my visit came to an end, I would think on the drive home that I couldn't wait until the next time I could drive down to visit Tom. Tom was failing and I was wanting to be there with him as much as possible and to be present for Jean and Tom's two children, Susannah and David.

TOM KIRSCH: A MAN FOR ALL SEASONS

As energized and vital as Tom's embrace of life could be, he also had the uncanny knack of dozing off on just about any occasion—a trait that we shared. I can't count the number of times when I was sitting in a boring meeting that both Tom and I were attending and note with increasing embarrassment that Tom's chin had dropped to his chest as he dozed off. Even more impressively, right in the midst of such a snooze, Tom would suddenly raise his head, make an insightful comment that was totally in step with what had just been said as if he hadn't missed a beat. In Tom's final weeks, I was visiting one day—sitting by Tom's bed as he was in such a snooze—when he suddenly lifted his head as Sam, a helper in the Kirsch household, walked into the room to say goodbye at the end of his workday. Always alert to what was most important to others around him, even in the last days of his life, Tom went straight from being sound asleep to congratulating Sam on the birth of his first grandchild. Sam beamed at Tom's recognition of this joyous event. Tom's unbelievably finely tuned feeling could work even when he was sound asleep and dying.

Tom was both sweet in an almost childlike way and a wise old man at the end. He had truly come full circle. Sometimes, I wasn't sure if I was speaking to the sweet child or the wise old man or both. On one occasion in those last days as I was sitting by his bedside, Tom became quite agitated and kept looking at his watch over and over again. Somehow, I knew that he wanted to know when he was going to die as he was a precise traveler and never missed a plane. But he was also a great baseball fan and I knew the Giants were playing a game that afternoon. Rather unbelievably, I found myself asking, "Tom, are you trying to figure out what time you are going to die or are you wondering when the Giant's baseball game starts on TV?" Again, without missing a beat, Tom said simply "BOTH." Tom could function on many levels simultaneously. This is not the same as multitasking. Rather, it is the capacity to seamlessly move back and forth from the mundane to the deep. Tom's perceptions and communications were natural, and simple—but the ease of his straightforwardness was deceptive in that he was also rooted in the complexities of the depths.

I don't really know what "individuation" means but I do know that Tom lived a remarkably full and complete life. I suggest that the reader view Luis Moris' 2016 Blue Salamandra film entitled "Thomas B. Kirsch in Conversation with Murray Stein." The film was produced in Jung's home in what turned out to be the last year of Tom's life. Most of the scenes take place in Jung's library. When I first viewed the film, I found myself reacting negatively as Tom and Murray Stein stiffly enter the formidable front doors of the house and awkwardly climb the dark stairwell to the second-floor library. It seemed so heavy and gloomy. But, as the film progressed, it got lighter and lighter. Murray and Tom have a lively exchange as they review so many aspects of Tom's life, thinking, and knowledge of the theory and practice of Jungian tradition over time. By the end of the film, it has become truly transcendent in the numinous glow of light that seems to shine through Tom's skin— as if one is viewing an inner light that infuses Tom's being. The conversation between Murray and Tom literally breathes life into Jung's library which seemed so dead when they first entered it.

Tom's fundamental modesty, quiet thoughtfulness, deep knowledge of the Jungian tradition, and direct, finely informed feeling shines through the film which, by the end, soars like the spirit. Murray Stein's sensitive and probing questioning allows Tom's exacting memory of people, places, and issues of different eras in his lifelong career as a Jungian to flow like the film's music and the occasional scenes of rippling streams of water—with a warmth and beauty that is both touching and enlightening. The film has a wonderful tone—in its color, in its conversation, and in its depth. If you want to know what Jung meant by "to rest in Tao means fulfillment, wholeness, one's destination reached, one's mission done," watch this film. Tom is at once sweet, disciplined and elegant. And, his loyalty was unshakeable. I view friendship as a rare treasure and friendship with Tom was a treasure's treasure.

From L to R: Thomas Singer, Craig San Roque, Thomas Kirsch.

Tom as a Feeling Mentor and Monitor
by John Beebe

I first met Tom Kirsch, in the summer of 1965, a few weeks after I had started my medical internship at the United States Public Health Service Hospital in San Francisco. That hospital, though no longer functioning as a health facility for members of the U.S. Merchant Marine and for people serving in the Coast Guard, is situated about halfway between my present home in San Francisco and the office in which I have practiced Jungian psychotherapy as a psychiatrist for the past forty-eight years. I pass by the building on the way to work several times each week, and not infrequently I reflect on how appropriate it is that it was there that I met Tom and began a friendship that, almost all by itself, took me fully half way to the professional life that I presently enjoy. If I may use myself as an example, it will be clear why I think Tom's special gift was the encouragement of others whom he recognized as destined to lead what he would call in his own autobiography "a Jungian life." How he did so is perhaps best approached by telling my own story.

I had gone to medical school at the University of Chicago with the explicit intention of becoming a psychiatrist, a vocation that had impressed itself upon me as mine on my 19th birthday, and that I had first confessed to the mother of a friend at Harvard, who, like me, was majoring in English and planning to become a writer. My friend's mother was herself a writer, but was very interested in psychiatry, because the pioneering American medical psychologist, Beatrice Hinkle, an early student of Jung's, had treated her for a long creative breakdown, so successfully that she held the record for the largest number of stories sold to *The New Yorker* in a single year—twelve! When I met her in the summer of 1957, I was just turning 18. She couldn't stop talking about her Jungian analysis, and the following year I began to volunteer at a mental hospital, which led to a continuous engagement with the kind of psychiatric patient that had made Jung realize the urgency of the psyche's need for the right kind of attention and care. By the summer of 1958, it was already clear to me that I too would need to devote a lifetime if I wanted to serve that need, and my friend's mother underscored that by telling me, "Well, if you want to be a doctor you can't be a writer," emphasizing the first and most important of the many sacrifices ahead.

So by the time I met Tom seven years later, I had already taken the first steps in the initiatory journey that I think entitled me to benefit from what he could add to my own deep commitment to a path similar to his, initially formed, in his case, by growing up within a psychotherapeutic family that had been shaped by its contact with Jung.

I knew what I wanted from Tom as soon as I met him: a referral to a psychotherapist for myself. At the University of Chicago, my mentor in thinking about what psychotherapy could be was not a physician, or even a member of the psychiatry department at the medical school, but a philosopher named Eugene Gendlin who was working in the psychology department, developing his own form of experiential psychotherapy based on an application of existentialism and phenomenology, and on practical work with Carl Rogers, in the time that Rogers was applying his technique of reflection of feeling to the revival of the self-process in schizophrenic adults. Gendlin taught me to think about psychotherapy as a process of developing understanding through the unpacking of felt meaning, and I was lucky enough to have four months of precious elective time working with him in the development of his "focusing" method. I was even included as a coauthor on the first published paper on that technique. I already had a way of talking to psychiatric patients in interviews when I first met Tom, and I think he saw that though I was naïve and more than a little inflated by the ideas I had learned, we had a lot in common.

I had decided (and told Eugene Gendlin, in one of our frequent phone calls that summer) that I would find a psychotherapist by asking the person who seemed most knowledgeable about psychotherapy for a referral. When the two full-time psychiatrists at the US Public Health Service Hospital, where I was doing a month's rotation in my internship seeing psychiatric patients, began talking about their new part-time colleague, Dr. Kirsch, whose primary job was with the National Institute of Mental Health evaluating psychiatric residencies around the country and who seemed to know just what was what about psychotherapy all over America, I decided that I would try to get to know this Dr. Kirsch. As he became one of my supervisors, the path to getting to know him was already at hand. Tom shared with me that he had taken a course in existentialism at Stanford, while a psychiatric resident there, and so we had the common ground of wanting to have a philosophy, as well as a practice, of therapy and to make a bridge between medical training and a liberal arts education. In those early conversations, Tom often pointed out to me that Jung was in fact a kind of philosopher. I recall him saying, "You know what a Jungian is? A Jungian is an existentialist who is interested in imagery." It was very meaningful to me that he had such a feeling for philosophy as relevant to clinical practice.

But I wanted Tom to give me a referral to a Rogerian therapist, thinking he must know one who was practicing in San Francisco. He said he didn't know one but would ask. Tom soon got back to me, telling me that a psychiatrist he knew who was particularly good with schizophrenic patients, John Perry, was close enough to Carl Rogers that Rogers stayed in his house when visiting Northern California. Perry, who at that time had the reputation of being "the best psychiatrist in San Francisco," as I learned from one of the merchant seamen I saw on the psychiatric service, seemed very likely the best bet for me, with my dual interest in Rogers and schizophrenia. Tom hoped I would accept him even though he was a Jungian. I was sure I wanted to do this, in an abstract way, but true to what I had learned from Gendlin, I was waiting for a felt sense that the time had come to act on the referral. I didn't know then that I might have waited forever, because introverted feeling is not only a very slow function of consciousness for me, but was carried by a trickster archetype that frequently put me in a double bind, paralyzing me from making connections I wanted, because a rather Magritte-like sentence would appear in my mind, "This is not the time," even when by every appearance the time, like Magritte's famous pipe, was at hand.

Fortunately, I had turned for help to Tom, and he asked more than once, "Have you called Dr. Perry yet?" Each time I'd say, I certainly plan to. The third time I said this, Tom had had enough; he had probably figured out that I was in a bind that someone else would have to untie. Tom has told the story in *A Jungian Life,* and I have no reason to contradict him:

> My one year at the US public health hospital was interesting both in terms of the interns I supervised and the kinds of patients I saw. Many of the patients were Merchant Marines, who were very different from Stanford students and faculty. I also supervised the interns going through the US Public Health Service training program. One intern I met then, John Beebe, has remained a lifelong friend. John knew a fair amount about Jung before he became a doctor, and during supervisory sessions with John I realized

that he was seeking analysis. I did something I've never done for anyone before or since: I actually telephoned John Perry and then handed the phone to John Beebe to make the appointment (Kirsch, 2014, p. 52).

This was not to be the only time that Tom helped me to enter the Jungian world. Five years later, I had finally come to the realization that beyond just wanting to be in analysis, I wanted to be an analyst myself. Refining my early motivation to become a psychiatrist to that degree of specificity as to the *kind* of psychiatric treatment I really wanted to be able to offer, and the recognition that that would be primarily Jungian, emerged not through identification, either with Tom or John Perry, but thanks to Dr. Perry's extraordinary, Rogers-like ability to mirror my tentative and indirect expressions of actual feeling about the kind of doctor I found myself wanting to become. I also had help from dreams that Dr. Perry listened to, but that I knew were my own. (These were the years of the Beatles, and I would often hear in my mind the words from "With a Little Help from my Friends," "What do you see when you turn out the light? I can't tell you, but I know it's mine.") Finally, in the summer of 1970, I saw myself riding a funicular railway in Switzerland that seemed to be "built on the architectural principle of id, ego, and superego." Nevertheless, as I finished the ride, a sign beside the place the train ended revealed that its actual name was the "C. G. Jung Railway." I knew then that I would be applying to the C. G. Jung Institute of San Francisco. I was at that time a second-year psychiatric resident at Stanford University Medical Center, and Tom, who was on the Clinical Faculty, was once more my psychotherapy supervisor. But I was still procrastinating; only this time I could tell Tom why. I had a same-sex erotic orientation, and I wasn't sure I would be welcome at any analytic Institute. I already knew that the Freudian psychoanalytic institutes were rejecting openly homosexual applicants and asking those who revealed their sexual orientations during training either to agree to strive toward heterosexuality or have their training terminated. This had happened to a friend of mine at two analytic institutes on the East Coast. The second time, he told me, he had rather cynically decided to time how long it would take the next Institute that accepted him to ask him to leave, once he revealed to his personal analyst that he was homosexual. He found out: 48 hours. Was the Jung Institute going to be different? I had to know. Once again, Tom came to the rescue. He said he didn't know, but would inquire of his own analyst, Joseph Henderson, who was on the admissions committee, whether there was any rule against a homosexual person applying. In a few days, Tom came back with the word, "There's no rule. It's how it fits into your life." And he agreed the matter should be discussed in the admission interviews.

To understand how remarkably helpful Tom's intervention was, one has to remember that in September 1970, when I applied to the Jung Institute of San Francisco, homosexuality was still listed as an illness in the American Psychiatric Association's diagnostic and statistical manual, homosexual acts between consenting adults were still illegal in California, and the Jung Institute had only recently incorporated itself as a nonprofit under California Law. There was no external reason to expect its admission committee to be other than cautious. I was later told that I was the first applicant who had been open about his or her sexual orientation in the admission interviews to be admitted to the Institute. I think the comfort I was able to evince during those interviews, thanks to Tom, had much to do with my being accepted the first time I applied.

What came next, in the evolution of my friendship with Tom, was my gradual realization that he had come to serve both as feeling mentor and feeling monitor to me, and that was holding me while my own analytic identity came into view. I had no idea how long he would function in that role. It turned out to be decades. Repeatedly, as I entered each next stage of my developing career, whether I was an analytic candidate, or a new analyst, or when publishing my first book written entirely under my own name (on that occasion Tom threw a party in my honor), Tom would reach out to me to help me find the right way to position myself in a feeling way toward the group in which I was gradually becoming visible. Tom did much to teach me about how not to be too intense, too idealistic, and too dominating. And at the end of his own career, he taught me by example how to give over with grace.

In the early years of the International Association for Jungian Studies, its member discussion list rather quickly became polarized. I would often try to balance the opposing points of view when I participated online. Although some appreciated my peacemaking efforts, I eventually began to suspect that I had become, as Judy Garland described her first husband, "irritatingly fair-minded," and admitted as much online. Immediately and privately, Tom congratulated me for this insight, adding, "John, I do feel that when you try to speak to both sides of an issue it can have a deadening effect." By now, I was in my sixties, when most people would have given up on me, but by reinforcing my realization in the timely and affirming way he did, Tom once again extended my professional life.

Along this long arc of our story, Tom probably influenced me most, once I got used to the fact that I was an analytic colleague and no longer Tom's pupil, through the example of his own extraordinary sensitivity to the international field that analytical psychology had become. Tom introduced me, for instance, to Shen Heyong, a year or so before I went to China for the first time in 1998 to speak at the First Conference on Analytical Psychology and Chinese Culture, which Dr. Shen organized. Tom recognized the need for experienced teachers of Jung who could foster the Jungian interest emerging in all parts of the world, teachers who would not inflate therapists who were first discovering the advantages of a Jungian identity and needed to recognize the power to do psychological harm that went with that. Tom had a wonderful way of coming into a country on any continent, meeting people there who were interested in Jung, and counseling them as to how to get their trainings started by getting as many outside advisers as possible. I think it is fair to say that the Developing Groups of Jungians, which were far fewer in number when he became President of the International Association for Analytical Psychology than now, would never have become the vital hubs they are today in so many parts of the world had Tom not encouraged particular individuals to get the kind of psychotherapy and accept the mentoring they would need to ground their own discoveries in a tradition. I know personally many people throughout the world who can say, just as I can, that the start of their working identities as Jungians owes everything to Tom's welcoming encouragement when they were just getting interested in Jung. Many of us would even say he gave us our lives, for Tom has also been a shaper of what Jungian identity means for those of us who started being Jungians in the 1970s or later. He provided a role model for how to live being Jungian in a contemporary professional way.

One way that Tom taught me to hold my place open to the rest of the Jungian world, rather than turn it into a concentration of power, came from some good advice he gave me about *The San Francisco Jung Institute Library Journal*. I had founded this journal, which began as a photocopied and stapled pamphlet, a year after I became a member analyst of the Institute and because of my bookish interests was made chair of its Library Committee. The Journal took a giant step forward in 1980, when a copy was placed on every seat at the Congress of the International Association for Analytical Psychology (IAAP), which was being held in San Francisco that year. Overnight, it became a quarterly publication read by Jungians all over the world and for a time had the largest circulation of any Jungian journal. During the early years of its international success, Tom was supportive of my efforts to keep the journal coming out under my protective editorship with the help of a tightly circumscribed Institute staff. But after a decade of success with this approach, Tom told me you are going to need next to do something you won't at first like: create an editorial board for the journal, so that "it's not just you." Although I had grown up as an only child, and was comfortable being one, I realized he was right, and for the next ten years I created such a board and finally was able to step down and watch the journal continue to evolve in extraordinary ways under four successive editors-in-chief, Steve Joseph, Dyane Sherwood (whose own editorial board renamed it *Jung Journal: Culture and Psyche* as she was getting it an academic publisher), Katherine Olivetti, and Jeffrey Benevedes, who have both brought it to new visual heights. Tom's envisioning that I needed to share the editing and management with others continues to benefit the *Journal*.

I think that many of Tom's greatest contributions to our field came in situations that involved the interface between Jungian organizations and the broader world. When he was President of the Jung Institute of San Francisco, he distinguished himself by convincing Robert Spitzer of the American Psychiatric Association that "Introverted Personality Disorder" was not an appropriate diagnosis for the Association to put into its Diagnostic and Statistical Manual, which in 1977 was still being revised to become DSM III. Tom's letter led Spitzer, at the last minute, to change his mind and use the term "Avoidant Personality Disorder" for the condition he wanted to name. This was a label that did not pathologize normal introversion. (Tom's role in keeping introversion from becoming a psychiatric diagnosis is told in the excellent book by Christopher

Lane, *Shyness: How Normal Behavior Became a Sickness*, p. 82.)

Within the IAAP, which he led as President for two three-year terms, his many ambassadorial efforts gave Tom a broader arena in which to exercise the caring embedded in his own introverted side, where a profound feeling for what was appropriate and needed, one auxiliary to his expansively outreaching dominant extraverted intuition, would often save the day. As President, Tom had to find a way to bring warring groups of Jungians together, or to be able to function separately in the same country, and he was often successful, as other Presidents of the IAAP have managed to be since him, tough as these situations become. I experienced first-hand, as an IAAP Member, how much long-term good Tom's introverted feeling could do.

In 1989, it came to light that the Analytical Psychology Club in Zurich had imposed a quota on Jewish members in January 1945. This was discussed at the IAAP Congress in Paris in August 1989, and I called for the Club to issue an apology. Tom, who was just about to start his second term as IAAP president, warned me that the Club might not apologize, since apologies for past actions, never popular in patriarchal cultures, were decidedly not seen as ideal within Swiss culture. The request for an apology was conveyed to a still living member of the Analytical Psychology Club's 1945 Executive Committee and to the Club's current president by Jerome Bernstein, who had been the Chair of the Workshop on Jung and Antisemitism at which the quota came to light. Three years later, at the next IAAP Congress in Chicago, Jerry Bernstein read with regret the letters he had received from the men he had written to, each of whom explained why he did not think the request was appropriate or within his authority to implement. Jane Reid, a member of the Analytical Psychology Club for decades, was at the Business Meeting of the IAAP where this was reported. She went up to Tom, as the Business Meeting was ending, to tell him she was upset. She informed him that the full membership of the Analytical Psychology Club had not heard of the request for an apology and that she for one would support a serious look at the issue. This conversation, which Tom held exquisitely, led to the Club agreeing to do an investigation that delivered not only an apology but also information no one had previously heard. They discovered that C.G. Jung had openly opposed a quota when it was first suggested in 1936, telling then Club members who feared undue influence from so many Jewish members who were relocating from Germany coming into the Club at once, that if the present Club members found these new members' influence unpleasant they should look for the causes of that reaction in themselves. I read the letter of apology from the Club at the Business Meeting of the 1995 IAAP Congress in Zurich. It had a definably healing effect.

None of this could have come to pass had Tom not, against his own initial reservation about asking for an apology, heard first me, then Jerry, and finally Jane in sequence, with a developing process of judgment leading to reappraisal and to establishing the value of allowing the Club to find its way to learn about what happened and what it needed to apologize for. No one else but Tom could have listened as well in a non-heroic way, allowing himself to be initiated into facilitating a satisfactory outcome through an evolving sense of where the power to effect change lay. This was an exquisite chronic crisis intervention, yet Tom did not take credit for what happened. There are now several accounts of the process involved (Bernstein, in Maidenbaum & Martin, 1991, pp. 319-331; Bernstein in Maidenbaum, 1992, pp. 117-127; Bernstein in Mattoon, 1991, 499-500; Mattoon 1997, pp 713-716; Kirsch, 2014, pp. 88-89) and the common thread is that though communications were often strained along the way, Tom's willingness to keep listening assured that a real resolution could occur. What Tom did was to hold the conflict so that an emergent process of repair that wanted to happen could occur. Few colleagues in Tom's position could have been as elegant in such a touchy situation.

Of course, I can also recall times that did not go as well, when Tom would be baffled by people unwilling to let him counsel them or to offer counsel to him when he asked for it. It must have felt to them like it was he who was unable to hear or see them. Tom's introverted feeling did not always sit well with people with strong introverted thinking. His wish to counsel them could feel gratuitous and injured pride sometimes impeded him from accepting and acknowledging input when they pointed out his thinking errors.

My own problem with Tom, when I had one, was of another order, and Tom's holding of me helped to heal it. I have had a hard time accepting love from father figures, and I never had an actual elder brother, so it moved me a lot, years into our mature years as analytic colleagues, when Tom said suddenly, "I love you," in a way that I could accept. I did not hurry to reciprocate the acknowledgment of our long bond. It was more important, I think for both of us, that I take in Tom's feeling. We were never a bromance, and we never had to endure a cooling off.

Was I ever able to help Tom when he was disappointed that other people could not accept what he had to offer? I think so. I think he responded well when I could help him see that they too had their own needs to mentor and father and protect. It is to Tom's eternal credit that he never refused a good idea from me, if it genuinely helped him to understand something. And I am so grateful he never stopped sharing his feeling with me when it included a judgment that in this or that situation I really had not been entirely appropriate.

The last time this happened was shortly before his death. I had chosen to arrange a minor thing that concerned Tom with Jean, without running it by him directly. I didn't want to bother him, since I knew he was dying. Tom, however, got upset that Jean and I were planning something that involved him without including him. Jean called me and tactfully conveyed his wish that I come in person to see him. I was planning to come to see him that week anyway, but I knew from his urgency that this could be our last chance. I came the very next day. While I sat facing Tom this final time, he was obviously happy that I was there. He told me he didn't understand why he'd become so upset. When it came time to leave, though, I debated whether I should kiss Tom on the forehead. After all, that forehead had often figured out what would be best for me. I wondered if he knew how much I loved it. Finally, though I decided I would just stay a bit longer. I had realized Tom would appreciate most seeing me able to sit there, holding the truth of our friendship without having to dramatize it. Our love for each other had always been intact. We had always stood by it, and we both knew It would take care of itself.

References

Kirsch, Thomas B. (2014) *A Jungian Life.* Carmel, CA: Fisher King Press.

Lane, Christopher. (2007). *Shyness: How Normal Behavior Became a Sickness.* New Haven: Yale University Press.

Maidenbaum, Aryeh and Martin, Stephen A. (Eds.) (1991) *Lingering Shadows: Jungians, Freudians, and Anti-Semitism.* Boston & London: Shambala.

Maidenbaum, Aryeh (Ed.) (2002) *Jung and the Shadow of Anti-Semitism.* Berwick, ME: Nicolas Hays, Inc.

Mattoon, Mary Ann (Ed.) (1991). *Paris 89: Proceedings of the Eleventh International Congress for Analytical Psychology,* Einsiedeln: Daimon Verlag.

Mattoon, Mary Ann (Ed.) (1997). *Zurich 95: Proceedings of the Thirteenth International Congress for Analytical Psychology.* Einsiedeln: Daimon Verlag.

Tom Kirsch in China
by Gao Lan[10], Heyong Shen[11]

At the opening ceremony of the 8th International Conference of Analytical Psychology and Chinese Culture in Chang'an University, Xi'an, China (April, 2018), we first introduced "Tom Kirsch and China" and then played a film with the title: "Called or not called, Tom Kirsch in China, Enlightenment and Individuation." More than 8,000 people attended this conference, the theme of which was "Enlightenment and Individuation." That's exactly the vivid portrait we have of Tom Kirsch in China.

Tom in China is one part of his life journey and it was his destiny. Tom and Jean Kirsch and Murray and Jan Stein started the formal development of IAAP in China 24 years ago. Today, its rich achievement leaves all a precious legacy.

We encountered Jungian analysis in the United States, and contacted Tom Kirsch and Murray Stein in 1993. Soon after that, we, joined with Professor Yan Zexian, the president of South China Normal University then, invited and arranged Tom Kirsch and Murray

---

[10] Gao Lan, professor of South China Normal University, distinguished professor of CityU.
[11] Heyong Shen, professor of City University of Macao, South China Normal University ⁞Corresponding Author ⌡

Stein's visit to China on behalf of IAAP in 1994 (with the help and assistance of Edward Low and his friend Yehua Zhu-Levine). We worked together for lectures and seminars in Guangzhou and Beijing, met Chinese scholars, psychologists and philosophers, and visited several important temples (both for Taoism and Buddhism), the Forbidden City, and the Great Wall. Since then, Tom and Murray became our mentors, for our personal process of Jungian training and for the development of analytical psychology in China.

Our first impression of Tom is as a seeker of Tao. His first speech in China at South China Normal University (1994) ." A week later, we went to Beijing, where Tom gave his second and third speeches at the first China National Conference of Psychotherapy and met with a Chinese psychologist. Tom spoke further on topics such as Synchronicity and I Ching, Individuation, and The Secret of the Golden Flower. Their visit was a special opportunity for Analytical Psychology and for Chinese culture. As Murray Stein wrote in his "Report on an IAAP Visit to China": "On August 11, 1994, we were visiting China at the formal invitation of Professor Yan Ze Xian, and of Dr. Shen Heyong... Last winter Dr. Shen had contacted me while he was studying in the United States and had invited us to visit him and his colleagues at the University in Guangzhou (Canton)... ...we come to China as representatives of IAAP, curious as to what we would find in this vast and ancient civilization, which is just now once again opening somewhat to the West and aware that this would be an historic event if the contact between Jungian psychology and the Chinese we were to meet turned out to be auspicious."[12] In fact, the visit by Tom and Murray to China planted the seed of IAAP in this ancient land, which is undergoing modernization.

In his lecture of the Tao and Jung, Tom expressed his open and warm heart to Chinese culture, as he explained the basic principles of Jungian psychology. According to Tom's understanding, Tao is the highest category of Chinese philosophy, covering Taoism, Confucianism, and Buddhism. It is also the most important enlightenment and contribution from East to Western psychology. Like *I Ching, the Book of Changes*, the Tao of China is also the "Archimedean Point" for analytical psychology. Such understanding is also C.G. Jung's point of view. Tom's presentations aroused great interest, both for analytical psychology and Chinese culture. As Murray recorded: "Tom presented a paper entitled 'Jung and Taoism,' in which he traced the influence of Taoist thought on Jung and drew some parallels between the theories of analytical psychology and Taoist philosophy. The audience (including myself) was surprised to hear from him that Jung had once claimed that Richard Wilhelm, who had guided Jung into some of the more subtle areas of Chinese thinking, had been a greater influence on him than Freud. It was through Wilhelm that Jung was effectively introduced to Chinese culture, to Chinese alchemy, and to the I Ching, all of which were deeply significant in his own thinking about the nature of the psyche."[13]

---

[12] Stein, Murray. (1995). Report on an IAAP Visit to China. IAAP Newsletter.
[13] Murray Stein, Report on an IAAP Visit to China. IAAP Newsletter, 1995

Many years later, When Tom Kirsch recalled his first visit to China over 20 years ago, in the interview of "Analytical Psychology in China" program, he was so grateful and satisfied. He said to the reporter: "For me, I lectured on Jung and his relationship to the East and China. I talked about I Ching. And what happened, a professor there, who told me that, 'Yes! Dr. Kirsch, you are right. What you tell us of Jung and Chinese culture is right. He understands the Chinese Psyche,' which was a big relief. And so, that was the beginning of Analytical Psychology in China."[14] Tom Kirsch wrote in the foreword to our Chinese version of *Jung and Analytical Psychology* in 2004: "One can speculate that it has to do with China's rich philosophical and religious traditions dating back 3,000 years. The wisdom inherent in Taoism, Buddhism, and Confucianism has given ample containment for the Chinese psyche throughout history. Many Western philosophers dating back to Leibniz, Schopenhauer, and more recently, Nietzsche, have been attracted to the philosophies of the East, mainly because they speak to the reality of the inner life and emphasize inner development."[15] When Tom's books were translated into Chinese, we wrote introductions for the readers: "True Spiritual History" for his *The Jungians: A Comparative and Historical Perspective* and for "Jungian's Life Road, Stay in the Hearts of the World" for his *A Jungian Life*.

---

[14] Tom Kirsch by interview. Ji Yuanjie. Analytical Psychology in China. Taiyan, Shanxi ChunQiu Electronic Audio-Visual Press 2018.
[15] Tom Kirsch, Forward to Heyong Shen's Jung and Analytical Psychology. Guangzhou, Guangdong High Education Press, 2004.

When planted by the heart, there must be gains. The planted seed, as Tom and Murray's visit in 1994, sprouted after a few years, as the first International Conference of Analytical Psychology and Chinese Culture in 1998. Luigi Zoja, the president of IAA then, said in his opening greetings: "It gives me immense pleasure to send you a message of greeting and support on this historic occasion. Jungian psychology has had a long and respectful relationship with China and its culture, and I am sure that Professor Jung himself would have been exceeding gratified to learn of the existence of such a conference as yours."[16] Since then, we have continued the work for eight conferences until 2018, and formed the IAAP Chinese regions, including Guangzhou, Hong Kong, Taiwan, Macao, Shanghai, and Beijing Developing Groups. Other developments since Tom and Murray's visit are that we have set up three institutes for analytical psychology in three universities (South China Normal University/Guangzhou, Fudan University/Shanghai, City University of Macao/Macao), and have translated the Collected Works of C.G. Jung (20 volumes), the Selected Works of C.G. Jung (nine volumes), and have published over 100 books by Jungian scholars, such as Tom Kirsch, Murray Stein, Luigi Zoja, Ruth Ammann, Kazuhiko Higuchi, Hayao Kawai, n, Marie-Louise von Franz, and Barbara Hannah. At the same time, we and our Chinese Jungian groups, have taken Jungian practice into life, set up 83 workstations

---

[16] Zoja, Luigi & Shen Heyong (Ed.). (2006). Opening Greetings for the First International Conference of Analytical Psychology and Chinese Culture. Psyche: Analysis and Experience, 5. Guangdong Education Press.

for the Garden of the Heart & Soul, using Analytical Psychology and Sandplay Therapy, to help the psychological development of orphans and to offer psychological relief for the victims of earthquakes.

In fact, Tom in China was not just for teaching and work, but also for life and culture in general. Tom told us several times that he loves China, he loves Chinese culture so much. We visited the historical sites in Guangzhou, Beijing, and Shanghai, for instance. What has interested Tom so much is the people, the Chinese people and their life. He enjoys Chinese art, music, Peking Opera, painting and calligraphy, Taiji movement, and Chinese foods.

In the summer of 2006, Tom visited with Steve and Jenny Zhang from Taiwan. During the lunch, Tom told us a story of his recent visit to Joe Henderson. They talked about the war and peace of the world today ... we were all touched by his story. Steve and Jenny Zhang decided to invite Tom and Jean to Taiwan. Tom and Jean happily accepted, and then, we had the formal development of IAAP in the region. Since then, Tom visited both Taiwan and mainland China almost every year.

At the 7th International Conference of Analytical Psychology and Chinese Culture (at the City University of Macao, 2015), Tom Kirsch gave the plenary speech. He started in this way: "This paper is a highly personal account of a series of traumatic events against the background of large political and cultural forces. The trauma of my birth occurred when Europe was in a state of chaos, and Hitler and the Nazis were becoming the dominant force on the European continent... My development of renal cell carcinoma and type 2 diabetes was also personally traumatic and exposed me to different cultural attitudes."[17] Tom used his personal traumatic experiences and reflections, responding to the theme of the conference, Confronting Collective Trauma: Archetype, Culture, and Healing. Tom's life journey is a Jungian life. The sufferings he experienced convey healing and self-knowledge to us all.

In July of 2017, the San Francisco C.G. Jung Institute organized a special training program for the Routers and candidates from the IAAP Chinese Region (Hong Kong, Taiwan, Macao, and the mainland of China): "The Theory and Practice of Jungian Psychotherapy, Explorations in the Unconscious." Tom, in his wheelchair, gave 5l lectures to the audience. On the last day of the training, Tom told us, the people from the Chinese region: "I am so grateful for your coming to San Francisco. As I could not visit China again, you coming to San Francisco made me so happy and grateful." We were all deeply touched by Tom, and we gave our heartfelt thanks.

Tom and Jean took us to meet Dr. Joe Henderson in 1997 during his birthday party at Mary Jo Spencer's house. We discussed the image of the 27 hexagrams of I Ching on the way from Palo Alto to San Francisco. Tom was very interested in this hexagram for its implied meaning of nourishment. As the image of "I" (the 27 hexagram, above keeping still, mountain; and below the arousing, thunder) showing us that nature nourishes all creatures. When the seed is planted in the earth, just as

---

[17] Kirsch, Tom. (2017). Plenary Speech at the 7th International Conference of Analytical Psychology and Chinese Culture. Macao.

Tom and Murray's first visit to China, all things are made ready for growth. According to the teaching of I Ching, this is an image of providing nourishment through movement and tranquility. The superior man takes it as a pattern for the nourishment and cultivation of his character. The image of the 27 hexagram I, relates to the hexagram 30 (The Clinging, Fire) and to 61 (the Inner Truth). In the hexagram 30, there is the image of the heart. And for the hexagram 61 conveys the symbolic meaning of heartfelt responding, for the inner truth. We brought our discussion, and the image of I to Dr. Joe Henderson. He was so happy, and accepted it as a birthday gift. We, with Dr. Joe Henderson, Mary Jo Spencer, John Beebe, and Adam Frey, shared the development of analytical psychology in China, and the meaning of the Psychology of the Heart.

Tom and Jean came to China often since their first visit in 1994. For a conference at Fudan University (2010), Tom gave a presentation on Jungian Individuation. Someone asked: "Could you simply answer the biggest difference between Freudian and Jungian psychoanalysis?" Tom looked at us, we sat beside him, and he turned to the questioner with smile: "The biggest difference is, as you asked, our Jungian analysts learn and understand I Ching." Even though it was a humorous answer, we were so happy to hear that from Tom.

We worked with Tom and Murray on the Roundtable of I Ching and Jungian Analysis at Qingdao, the city where Richard Wilhelm lived for more than 20 years. Bettina Wilhelm (the granddaughter of R. Wilhelm), Christa Robinson, John Beebe, John Hill, Paul Brutsche, Liu Dajun and some Chinese I Ching scholars attended.

Tom told the story of C.G. Jung and Richard Wilhelm, the translation of I Ching, the Rainmaker, and The Secret of the Golden Flower. In the discussion, Tom especially mentioned and quoted from a letter Jung wrote to Wilhelm: "Fate seems to have apportioned to us the role of two piers which support the bridge between East and West,"(May 25, 1929)[18] and also Jung's description of his meeting with Richard Wilhelm, "there the spark leapt across and kindled a light that was to become for me one of the most significant events of my life. Because of this I may perhaps speak of Wilhelm and his work, thinking with grateful respect of this mind which created a bridge between East and West and gave to the Occident the precious heritage of a culture thousands of years old, a culture perhaps destined to disappear forever."[19] Both Tom and Murray, agreed that the task that C.G. Jung and Wilhelm started, we must continue.

Because of Tom and his Chinese heart, the San Francisco C.G. Jung Institute held an international conference with the theme: "Jung and China," at the San Francisco Chinese museum in 2014. Tom chaired our speeches and began with this description: "After I visited China, I realized how important Chinese culture is for our Jungian psychology. Even though I am so familiar with Jung's works, his *Memories, Dreams, Reflections*, for instance, it's through my experience in China, my conversions with Heyong and Gao Lan, I had new realizations about Jung's relationship with Tao. I am so

---

[18] Jung, C.G. (1973). *Letters*. Selected and edited by Gerhard Adler. Vol.1: 1906-1950, 66. N.J.: Princeton University Press.
[19] Jung, C.G. *Richard Wilhelm: In Memoriam*. CW 15. § 74

touched by his last paragraph of Retrospect: "When Lao-tzu says: 'All are clear, I alone am clouded,' he is expressing what I now feel in advanced old age. Lao-tzu is the example of a man with superior insight who has seen and experienced worth and worthlessness, and who at the end of his life desires to return into his own being, into the eternal, unknowable meaning. The archetype of the old man who has seen enough is eternally true … the more uncertain I have felt about myself, the more there has grown up in me a feeling of kinship with all things. In fact, it seems to me as if that alienation, which so long separated me from the world, has become transferred into my own inner world and has revealed to me an unexpected unfamiliarity with myself."[20] Then Tom read the paragraph loudly, for the start of the "Jung and China" international conference.

We spent the day with Tom and Jean on July 16, 2017. We didn't want to go out for lunch, just to stay in the house to continue our visit and conversation with Tom. Our personal analysis is so closely related to Tom, as it started in Palo Alto. Tom shared his family stories about his father and mother, his experience with C.G. Jung, and his analyst, Joe Henderson. Before we left, Tom tried to stand up from the chair. He told us he loves China, loves the Chinese culture, and Tao.

Three days before Tom Kirsch passed away on October 19, 2017, Heyong had a dream: "[in the dream] Tom and I visited three boys [it looked like it was in a special hospital]. Tom brought some food to them. Then

---

[20] Jung, C.G. (1989). *Memories, Dreams, Reflections*, 359. New York: Vintage Books.

Tom and I went home. Three dogs were before us, and one of the dogs went underground. There was a young girl in the home [Tom's daughter], and she just wanted to go outside by herself. She left in a hurry on my bicycle. At the end of the dream, I stood at the gate of the place, opened a box on the door, and inside were several bags. I touched each of the bags, and inside the bags may have been some herbs [I felt that they related to Tom]. I was feeling lonely and lost at that moment, and then I woke up."

Three days later, when the sad news came, we burned incense for Tom, and chanting Chu Ci Zhao Hun (Summoning the Soul, by Quyuan). We wrote a memorial essay at the day, sent to our members of Chinese Developing Groups. A few days later, we wrote a letter to Jean and mentioned the dream. Jean wrote back to us: "Your dream touched me deeply... With your dream you responded from the depths of your cultural unconscious ... with the image of Hun and Po... [And the number symbolism] suggests to me that your dream reaches deeper, even, than the antiquity of Chinese Taoist philosophy, to the true collective unconscious..." Jean continued in her letter: "It seems so "Tom-like" to me, that in your dream one of the dogs (Hun) goes into the earth. Tom was always so solid when it came to human relationships, never speaking metaphysics; but I knew from living close to him that he "believed"—or, as Jung did, that he "knew" the [reality of the] forces beyond understanding. He was thoroughly "grounded" as a human being, and he was almost always accurate in his reading of other people's feeling states... I believe that he was receptive to all the energies that were generated by people around the globe who knew him and cared about him. I have observed many deaths in my almost 80 years and no one has ever made that great transition before my eyes and under my hand with greater peace and ease. Susannah, David, his wonderful caretaker Ana, and I held his hands and stroked his body as he breathed his last, quietly and with great dignity."[21]

The program and organizing committees of the 8th International Conference of Analytical Psychology and Chinese Culture decided to have a special memorial for Tom Kirsch at the opening ceremony of the conference. Jean wrote a letter to us on March 18, 2018, especially for the conference. In the letter, Jean says, "Tom would be profoundly moved, were he to know how you are honoring him today. I can imagine his childlike delight—simple and direct and joyful—in response to your remembrance! It would bring tears to our eyes." Jean told us a story about Tom in the letter: "I recalled what Tom had said to me one evening over dinner, when I had suddenly become tearful at the thought of fulfilling his wishes to be cremated and to scatter his ashes at sea. "But where will I go to find you, to talk to you when I miss you?" Tom had looked down at his hands for a long moment and then raised his head and said brightly, "Look for me in people!" Jean continued in the letter: "We can find him within ourselves. We can listen for the Tom that we know, who still lives in us, who still speaks to us in our memories and dreams. And we can share the Tom we know with one another. I believe he would like that very much." At the end of the letter, Jean says:

---
[21] Letter from Jean Kirsch, 31, October 2017.

"Thank you, Gao Lan and Heyong, for all that you and your students have done and continue to do, to further an understanding of the psyche and to build bridges between individuals and cultures. That is a perfect way to honor Tom."[22]

Heyong and Joe Cambray, co-chaired the opening ceremony of the 8th International Conference of Analytical Psychology and Chinese Culture. The conference was held in Chuang'an University (Chuang'an is the old name for Xian city, which means "long peace") of China, from March 31 to April 4. For the Sunday of April 1, is the same as Easter Day. April 5 is the Chinese Qing Ming Festival, All Souls' Day. It's really synchronicity. We took the Delphic oracle carved on the door of C.G. Jung's house in Kusnacht, "Called or not called, God will be

Tom Kirsch, Gao Lan, Jean Kirsch, and Heyong Shen, at the Island for Washing of the Heart, 2010

---

[22] Letter from Jean Kirsch, March 18, 2018.

A JUNGIAN LEGACY

Murray Stein, Jean Kirsch, Bettina Wilhelm, John Beebe, Heyong Shen, and Tom Kirsch, at Richard Wilhelm's old house in Qingdao, 2013

The 2018 opening ceremony of the 8th International Conference for Analytical Psychology and Chinese Culture, which began with the film: "Calling or not, Divine forever: Tom Kirsch in China, Enlightenment and Individuation."

there" (VOCATUS ATQUE NON VOCATUS DEUS ADERIT) for the theme of the film and for the memorial of Tom Kirsch. Tom in China, is one part of his life journey, a Jungian life. He planted the seed of IAAP in China. It has sprouted with the IAAP Chinese region today. The theme of the Conference: "Enlightenment and Individuation," is precisely the witness and embodiment of the spirit and legacy of Tom Kirsch.

Tribute to Tom Kirsch
by Andreas Jung

Gateway to the World

Tom and I first met in August 1995 at the opening ceremony of the 13th Congress of the IAAP in Zurich. We probably shook hands without taking further notice of each other. A few days later my father phoned me at my office, asking if I would join them for a cup of coffee in the nearby Bahnhof Buffet, Zurich. There I found my father and a kind man in his prime: the president of the IAAP, Thomas Kirsch! We exchanged some friendly words, but soon I had to go back to my work, the preservation of monuments in the city.

Ten years later Murray Stein, with whom I got acquainted not long before, invited my wife, Vreni, and me for lunch at the traditional Veltliner Keller in the Old Town of Zurich. There, Murray introduced us to his wife, Jan, and to Tom and Jean Kirsch, who had come from California. Together we enjoyed a lovely meal. As Jean confessed much later, she was afraid of being forced to attend an awkward business event. But one word led to another and after a short while we became aware that we shared a similar kind of odd dry humor, and our group turned to a cheery company of almost old friends.

But the main reason for our meeting was a different story. The befriended couples had set themselves the goal of bringing a living Jung family member to the United States of America! Although being "real Jungs" we did not feel like crossing the wide Atlantic Ocean considering our advanced age. What actually would they expect me to do? It was to attend the 4th History Symposium in San Francisco in 2006 and to give a public interview, share some private memories, or lecture about a specific topic of my choice.

Not being psychologist, I wondered what I could contribute. As an architect, I probably should speak about the House C.G. Jung in Küsnacht. Only later I realized that the subject of the conference was "Jung and Religion" – good heavens! But all of a sudden, the motto of my grandfather came to my mind: VOCATUS ATQUE NON VOCATUS - DEUS ADERIT: "Called or not called, God will be there." That was the answer. Now I knew the title of my talk!

I prepared an elaborate lecture with many pictures presenting the house and C.G. Jung as builder. Doing this, I was wondering if my grandfather would agree to some of my conclusions. The last day before departure I finished my talk. To relax, I inserted a CD Vreni had got that very day in a fashion store and pressed the button of my computer: "VOCATUS ATQUE NON VOCATUS - DEUS ADERIT: those are the words written on the lintel of my house in Küsnacht...". Vreni and I looked at each other as if we had seen a ghost and listened spellbound—this was unmistakably the voice of my grandfather—thank God, Grandpa gave his blessing! Only much later I found that the coincidence was due to an involuntary handling, stirring up a forgotten file in the computer.

In San Francisco we had a wonderful time. One day we took the train to Palo Alto, where Tom Kirsch awaited us at the station. He drove us to Stanford University and showed us around the huge campus with all its amazing buildings. After that we went to the Kirsch's home where we were served an excellent dinner and met with their friends from the Jung Institute of San Francisco. With many of them we also became friends over time. It was a very warm and inspiring evening. Next afternoon, director Baruch Gould drove us to Fort Mason Center and helped to install the technical equipment. I had to give the evening keynote. Tom introduced me in calm and simple words. The audience was attentive and favorable. After my lecture an elderly lady came towards me and confided that having attended my lecture, she now believed that Jung had really existed—before she assumed that Jung was probably just a dream...

Tom Kirsch opened the Gate to the World for us!

In the Course of Time

In October 2009, we again crossed the Ocean, since C.G. Jung's legendary *The Red Book* would be released in New York. That was the final peak of many years of persuasion within the family and meticulous work in the archives of the world. Vreni and I decided to attend this spectacular event, although we were worried about its impact in the newspapers and among the public.

Our start turned out to be rather difficult. Vreni was suffering from a persistent flu and therefore exhausted, and my cousin, Ulrich Hoerni, co-editor of *The Red Book*, also felt ill. We had accommodations in the Excelsior Hotel near Central Park. Fortunately, Tom happened to be there as well! It took him not long to find out where help was available. Quickly, he went to the nearest pharmacy, bought Vitamin C and prescribed Vreni a fourfold dosage! That way he helped her to withstand the challenging next hours and days. But also, he led all of us to the lovely Cafe Lola with its delicious cakes to awaken the spirits! We had a very good and inspiring time in New York. People were caring and we felt welcome!

We met Tom later again in Washington, D.C., in June 2010. The Library of Congress created an impressive exhibition on *The Red Book* connected with a profound symposium, where Tom was one of the speakers. We also had the pleasure to share Tom's lovely and inspiring birthday dinner at the Old Ebbit Grill.

Whenever Tom and Jean came to Switzerland, they would visit us, once accompanied by their daughter, Susannah, and granddaughter, Hildy, and always we had a great time together. We live on the shore, and Tom brought his swimsuit along, since he was delighted to swim in the Lake Zurich.

We were hoping to meet Tom again in Küsnacht or occasionally on prospective conventions somewhere in the world, but increasing health problems prevented him from traveling. So, with a heavy heart Tom had to renounce the participation in the Jung-Neumann Conference in 2015 in Israel. In consequence, he was connected via video, live on the wall of Kibbutz Shefayim. Tom's head appeared filling the entire screen—the presiding father figure—and in before him, all the real attendees sat as small as dwarfs! We had the possibility to talk to each other, but he looked tired and spoke slowly.

Door to the past

All the greater was the joy when Tom and Jean announced they would be coming to Switzerland in 2016! They arrived prior to the June 6 celebration of the 55th C.G. Jung Memorial Day. Tom held a most remarkable lecture, "Jung's Influence in the Arc of My Life," at ISAP-Zurich. He was the "old Tom" we knew: wise and witty, humble and humorous, fair and fascinating! He introduced in a clear and insightful manner the path of his life as a psychiatrist and his approach to Jung and the analytical psychology. It was most revealing and moving.

The next day, June 7, Tom Kirsch and Murray Stein rang the bell at Seestrasse 228 Küsnacht, the former home of C.G. Jung. Living here, I had the privilege to open the front door and invite them in. Already in position, filmmaker Luis Moris with his cameraman was prepared to capture the moment. Together, we went upstairs into Jung's Library and arranged everything for the intended film recordings. Sitting in front of the time-honored bookshelves, Tom recounted in a lively conversation with Murray Stein frankly his long and dedicated life. Those hours resulted in a beautiful film, still available.

Vreni and I had the pleasure to have the Kirschs over for dinner the next evening and to discuss the happenings of the past days and to exchange thoughts.

One important topic, of course, was the state of his health and the strain of travelling. But we still enjoyed a bright and lively evening.

On June 23, Tom and Jean invited us in turn to the Gothic Tavern of the old guild house, Rüden, in Zurich, where we had another pleasant meal together. We knew that it was probably the last time Tom would come over to Europe, and the chance of a future reunion was very small. Nonetheless, the table was in a cheerful mood and we all enjoyed the social gathering. Suddenly Tom's mobile rang: "Hello, this is the dentist, we would like to remind you of your appointment!". We broke out into a hearty laugh!

Tom and Jean had a flight back to San Francisco the next day. In the travel bag they carried the Swiss chocolate truffles we gave them and they liked so much, and back at home they twice reported how many of them were left.

Tom knew about my forthcoming admission to the IAAP in autumn and felt sorry to miss the International Congress in Kyoto. The following year was, according to Tom's words, very difficult with the steadily growing cancer. We still had some valuable talks on the phone. Although very ill at that time, his voice sounded firm and clear, and he seemed calm and to a certain point confident.

On October 22, 2017, we got the sad message: Tom died after midnight, gently and peacefully!

We have lost a dear and warm-hearted friend, an upright man with an unerring sense of personal integrity.

We think of him with thankfulness and esteem.

Andreas and Vreni Jung, July 28, 2018

Loving Tom, Living Tom, Losing Tom—A *Bricolage*
by Andrew Samuels

Explanation

When I received the invitation from Luis Moris to contribute to this book, I must confess my heart sank. I felt that I had written so much that I truly had nothing more to say that I would want to be out there in the public sphere. I was minded to say no.

But then I decided to take a risk and offer Luis three pieces that I had written during Tom's terminal illness and after his death. A *bricolage*, in fact. Wikipedia tells us that a *bricolage* is the construction or creation of a work from a diverse range of things that happen to be available. But the definition goes on to say that *Bricolage* is a French loanword that means the process of improvisation in a human endeavor. If there are a few repetitions, let them stand!

Right after Tom's death

I sent this out to two Jungian Google Groups—the International Association for Jungian Studies and also the Analysis and Activism group under the auspices of

IAAP. To my surprise, it was then forwarded to all the members of the C.G. Jung Institute of San Francisco and both Jungian institutes in Küsnacht and Zurich.

Dear Jungian Friends and Colleagues,

I have to let you know that our colleague and friend Tom Kirsch has died at his home in Palo Alto, California, after a long illness, aged 81.

[This is just an informal and personal message and there will be more official communications in due course, of that I am sure.]

Even though many of us knew this was coming, it does hurt a lot.

Tom was a big man, of greater stature in human and in professional terms than he sometimes allowed himself to know. I tried when we spoke during the last year, and the other day in Palo Alto, to let him know that he is the true architect of the contemporary Jungian world and that the community owes him a great deal. We have benefited from his numerous innovations and his success in modernising analytical psychology. For these achievements, he is recognised and remembered.

Without his support, the International Association for Jungian Studies and the Analysis and Activism project would perhaps never have come into being. The growth of Jungian analysis worldwide stems to a great extent from his founding vision.

Tom travelled extensively and one thing I feel noteworthy is that he always familiarised himself as deeply as possible with the local political situation, making sure that the development of the field was

LOVING TOM, LIVING TOM, LOSING TOM—A BRICOLAGE

congruent with the traditions and the changes in each country that he visited.

Tom was also no slouch intellectually and in terms of publication. One thinks of the *Selected Works*, his *Memoir*, the ground-breaking *The Jungians*, and the edited book of papers on *The Red Book*. This is a substantial oeuvre that will last. You can find these works on Amazon, of course.

But most of all I personally will remember such a dear friend, mentor, older brother and partner in crime. The warmest and most related man I have ever met. Why, who else in such a grave and mortal condition would remember what I had always liked over the years, and offer me the use of the hot tub when I arrived at the house?

To say again, this is just me writing. More will undoubtedly come.

Warmest wishes and love to you all,
Andrew

Contribution to Tom's memorial meeting

This was a unique event, with maybe 15 speakers given several minutes each to conjure up Tom. You can see that I was already finding it difficult to say anything new.

This is the fourth time I have written or spoken about Tom Kirsch since his death. I don't want to reprise in detail my earlier comments about his warmth and finely tuned feeling. I wrote earlier that Tom was "the most related man I have ever met."

Nor do I want to expand on what the loss of one of my closest friends of forty years means. Like Tom Singer, my emotions are quite visceral – I so miss the booming "Aaaaaaandrew" at the start of a phone call or encounter. Or the times in the hot tub together.

Instead, I seek to break some new ground for me by speaking of Tom in terms of his courage, in terms of his intellect, and in terms of his beauty. Courage. Intellect. Beauty.

Courage first. It took great personal courage to wake the International Association for Analytical Psychology from its slumbers and gently but firmly push it towards an engagement with the world. By "the world," I really do mean that Tom was the one who literally made us an *international* organization in any fullness. Jean was often by his side as an indispensable ally in what was a revolution.

When he died, so many messages came in about the role that Tom—sometimes with Jean—played in the development of analytical psychology in their country: Russia, Brazil, Korea, South Africa, Taiwan, China, to name a selection. Today, everyone celebrates the globalization of Jungian analysis.

But at the time—and I was there, serving under him on the IAAP committee—the opposition was *lurid*. Some said Tom just wanted to fly to exotic parts on the IAAP credit card. Others felt that this geo-extraversion was an inflation that would ruin the organisation. Tom rightfully held his position, and this took courage.

Once, this aspect of his courage became rather physical. It was at the time in 1993 when Boris Yeltsin had not completely consolidated his power and there were tanks outside the Russian Parliament, Moscow in uproar. Tom had a meeting planned with the prospective Russian publishers of the *Collected Works*. He called me and said "Shall I go?" I said, "No, are you crazy? It will be dangerous. The Foreign Office is telling Brits not to go there." Well he went, and it was crazy—but also incredibly brave.

Now for Tom's intellect. When Tom's intellect is under discussion, there has been a tendency to underestimate this part of his personality and life. "Not a thinking type," blah-blah-blah. And all of us who knew him well heard that his Dad did not credit him with much intelligence. This, I have to say, was total bullshit. I don't mean that Tom merely had emotional intelligence or something softer like that. No—Tom's intellectual output contains more than a few crunchy, important, innovative, and scholarly elements. Read his *Selected Works*. It was a great relief to me that we, at Routledge, burning the midnight oil, were able to bring the book out in half the usual time so that Tom could hold it in his hands and place it on a display stand where he could see it whenever the wanted to.

In that book, you will find his paper linking brain studies and REM sleep to dreaming. It was one of the first neuropsychological papers to appear in our field. His studies of training processes were full of sociocultural insights. And his book *The Jungians* was magisterial and remains the canonical text in relation to our history. Tom immersed himself in the wider politics of each country he surveyed as an indispensable base for his review of the Jungian politics.

How anyone can believe that a history carried out like that is not an irreducibly intellectual pursuit beats me.

Finally, beauty. Tom's physical presence is not something that has been much noticed. But let us never forget that this was a gorgeous man with a beautiful body. I think these attributes played a significant part in his rise to the positions of leadership that we all know about. Not all political leaders are beautiful, but some are—and Tom was.

It was a beauty that didn't vanish even on his deathbed. I am not talking about an ethereal or spiritual beauty here, but something gravelly, down to earth, of the flesh.

To draw this to a conclusion, after my words on Tom's intellect and beauty, I return to the question of his courage with these words from Dr. Martin Luther King, Jr.:

"The ultimate measure of a man is not where he stands in moments of comfort and convenience, but where he stands at times of challenge and controversy."

Foreword to Jungian Analysis, Depth Psychology and Soul: The Selected Works of Thomas B. Kirsch

Tom asked me to write this Foreword and to make it as much of an introduction and overview as possible. He also said I could be personal. Even without the book in your hand, you can get the breadth and depth of its contents. The passage critiquing psychoanalysis was the distillation of years of conversation between us about

LOVING TOM, LIVING TOM, LOSING TOM—A BRICOLAGE

how the relationship between analytical psychology and psychoanalysis was running off the tracks.

I am delighted and honoured to have been asked to contribute a Foreword to Thomas Kirsch's *Selected Works*. He is one of core creators of the Jungian world as we find it today. His knowledge of the history, the issues and the personalities is second to none. We Jungians know that Tom is kind, empathetic, related—and responsible for a raft of interesting publications never before gathered into one book. Maybe we overlooked how penetrating and controversial an observer of professional political process he is. At points in the book, he can be said to have taken no prisoners.

I entered the Jungian world in 1974 and I first met Tom at the Rome Congress of the International Association for Analytical Psychology (IAAP) in 1977. I asked him a question about his presentation, and the consequent friendship stuck so that we easily talked about ourselves as "older brother" and "younger brother." Later, I served under him on the Executive Committee of the IAAP, and was often employed as an emissary or even as a sort of fixer. He was a remarkable President who foresaw the global possibilities for analytical psychology.

It is not surprising that I have got to know his work pretty well. But I had never imagined it presented chronologically, and I think that this is a fortuitous feature of a collection that will appeal to analysts, candidates, academics and students.

When reading these chapters, it is possible to see how the world of professional politics and history, and the world of psychological theorising interweave. That is, Tom has taken his roles as professional leader and chronicler of analytical psychology and turned them into platforms for serious theory making. This approach is exemplified in his book *The Jungians: A Comparative and Historical Perspective* (2000).

In this book, the several chapters on training effectively demonstrate this interweave. Always aware of the present moment in training, Tom's various contributions preserve the classical Jungian core but relate openly to the changes going on in psychotherapy internationally as it developed into a profession, often modelled (sadly) on medicine. The passages on the dynamics of training in Chapters 2, 4, and 11 should be required reading for trainees and candidates—maybe even before they start to attend the seminars and lectures. In these chapters, we see another feature of this book: Tom's humanity, generosity, and flexibility. He accepts that, given the multifarious dynamics of the training community, "shit happens," and he is open about what he has witnessed in this regard. For Tom, "the wounded healer" is always already present in anything to do with depth psychology. It is much more than a question of fucked-up analysts.

Tom's historical work on the growth and spread of analytical psychology brings a crucial international perspective to the book. Either "Tom was there" or he knew someone well who was there. The result is that we have now got a history of our field of analytical psychology that addresses the questions surrounding its founders but does not at all stay on an anecdotal level. Indeed, when writing about the locales in which analytical psychology took root, Tom is remarkably sensitive to the cultural and even the socio-political situation that existed.

In this regard, Tom's style of writing reminds me of analysis itself. We now know that there is no "inner world" in a vacuum, sequestered from the society in which the participants in the process are situated. Moreover, you have to remember that the small details, the little character outlines, are in fact of the greatest importance. In a sense, analysis and psychotherapy involve a great deal of gossip which is often what really matters in a profession like this one. You can see this at moments in Chapters 5, 6, and 8.

Tom's parents were both famous Jungian analysts and this gave Tom access to things Jungian at a very young age. He grew up in the Jungian community. The personal disadvantages of this are obvious and can be taken for granted. But the advantages are considerable and often not as easily appreciated. For example, in Chapter 7, I, for one, learned things about Jung's close colleague and companion Toni Wolff as a person and as a professional that were brand new for me. This was solely because Tom had been able to examine the correspondence between his father and Wolff (Kirsch's father had been in analysis with both Jung and Wolff). What we read there about dream interpretation, and also on the need for discretion in professional life will repay attention.

I think that many who write about their "ancestors" are, covertly, writing about the present and the future as well. Readers can check this out for themselves by reading Tom's memoir, *A Jungian Life* (2014). When Tom writes about the Jungian "diaspora" in Chapter 6, he is, of course, chronicling the fate of those Jewish Jungian analysts who left Europe to avoid perishing in the Shoah. But the expansion of Jungian analysis into what used to be called "frontier zones," such as Russia, Latin America, and the Far East is also a kind of diaspora. So, when you read about the analysts who spread Jungian analysis because of their very peril, it is worthwhile to consider how today's expansionist dynamics resemble some of those that were in play in the 1930s.

In many of the chapters, there are passages that demonstrate Tom's prowess as a clinical writer, and some of them played a significant role in conveying to the non-Jungian clinical world several important things about how Jungians practice. For Tom, Jungian analysis and psychotherapy seem to occupy a middle position in today's spectrum of therapies. At one end of the spectrum, we see the tough therapies, the ones claiming to be based on science and on evidence. Tom is not averse to such modes of working though it is not where his clinical heart is. He is a quintessentially relational practitioner, with a fine understanding of images and symbols, as well as the therapy relationship. Yet—and this, I know, is important to Tom—at no point does he collapse his way of working into an ersatz psychoanalysis. It is different.

Thinking more about psychoanalysis (and maybe this is true about a wider range of today's therapies as well), there has been a "relational turn." Jung's standing as a pioneer of relational approaches is gradually being recognized. This is a serious strength. Like today's relational theorists, Jung asserted that analysis involved mutual transformation and was a "dialectical process."

LOVING TOM, LIVING TOM, LOSING TOM—A BRICOLAGE

Analysis for Jung, just as it is for the relationals, is "an encounter, a discussion between two psychic wholes in which knowledge is used only as a tool" (1935, p. 7). Jung goes on to say that the analyst is a "fellow participant in the analysis." His focus was often on "the real relationship," making his point in unmistakable terms: "In reality everything depends on the [person] and little on the method" (1931, p. 7). All of these themes are present in Tom's clinical writings.

To conclude, I want to make reference to Tom's considerable communicative talents as a teacher and lecturer. Tom is a brilliant teacher who touches people's feelings very deeply. To say this is important given that many of the chapters began life as lectures. To my eye and ear, the fact that the material reads as if it were being spoken is a huge strength. (The great Jungian analyst James Hillman once told me that to make one's writing sound as if it were spoken was a triumph!) I do realize that others might find the informality difficult to assimilate. But they should try! For this genre is one way of combining thought and emotion, intellect and soul.

London, January 2017

References

Jung, C.G. (1931). Commentary on The Secret of the Golden Flower. In *Collected Works*, Vol. 13.

Jung, C.G. (1935). Principles of practical psychotherapy. In *Collected Works*, Vol. 16.

Kirsch, T. (2000). The Jungians: A Comparative and Historical Perspective. London and New York: Routledge.

Kirsch, T. (2014). *A Jungian Life*. Carmel, CA.: Fisher King Press.

About the Author

Luis Moris is a Jungian analyst in private practice in Zurich. He is the founder of Blue Salamandra Films. He has produced and directed several films including interviews with prominent Jungian analysts.
Website: www.luismoris.com.

Lightning Source UK Ltd.
Milton Keynes UK
UKHW020738280921
391304UK00007B/116